Cover design by: Garry Martin

Unmasking Narcissism

Empowering Strategies to Navigate and Heal from Narcissistic Abuse

Chapter 1: Introduction

Definition of narcissism and narcissistic personality disorder (NPD).

*I*n this opening chapter, we delve into the complex world of narcissism *and Narcissistic Personality Disorder (NPD), shedding light on the defining characteristics that shape these conditions.*

Narcissism, at its core, is a psychological concept characterized by an excessive preoccupation with oneself, a grandiose sense of self-importance, and a profound need for admiration from others.

Narcissistic Personality Disorder, identified in the Diagnostic and Statistical Manual of Mental Disorders (DSM-5), represents a more extreme manifestation of narcissistic traits.

Individuals with NPD display a pervasive pattern of self-centeredness, an exaggerated sense of entitlement, a lack of empathy, and an insatiable desire for control and power over others.

To truly understand narcissism, we explore the origins and development of this complex personality trait.

While the exact causes of narcissism remain a subject of ongoing research, various factors such as genetics, early childhood experiences, and environmental influences have been implicated.

By unraveling the multifaceted nature of narcissism, we gain a deeper comprehension of its impact on both individuals and their relationships.

As we embark on this journey of unmasking narcissism, it is crucial to approach the topic with sensitivity, empathy, and a desire to empower individuals who have experienced narcissistic abuse.

Throughout this book, we will equip you with powerful strategies to navigate the treacherous waters of narcissistic relationships and provide comprehensive guidance on healing and reclaiming your life.

Please note that the information provided in this chapter is based on extensive research and professional expertise in the field of psychology.

It is essential to consult with qualified professionals for a formal diagnosis or specific therapeutic interventions related to narcissism and Narcissistic Personality Disorder.

Overview of the book's purpose and structure.

Welcome to the captivating journey of unmasking narcissism and empowering strategies to navigate and heal from narcissistic abuse.

In this chapter, we provide a comprehensive overview of the purpose and structure of this book, allowing you to understand the valuable insights and empowering guidance that lie ahead.

The primary purpose of this book is to shed light on the enigmatic world of narcissism, unraveling its complexities and providing a deeper understanding of Narcissistic Personality Disorder (NPD) and its impact on individuals and their relationships.

Through the exploration of narcissism, we aim to empower those who have experienced narcissistic abuse, equipping them with effective strategies to navigate these challenging dynamics and embark on a healing journey towards reclaiming their lives.

The structure of this book is carefully designed to provide a holistic approach to handling narcissists and healing from narcissistic abuse.

Each chapter delves into different aspects of narcissism and its effects, offering in-depth insights, evidence-based knowledge, and practical strategies to facilitate personal growth and transformation.

As we embark on this journey together, you can expect to explore the origins and development of narcissism, gaining a deeper comprehension of the various factors that contribute to its formation.

We will explore the defining traits and diagnostic criteria of Narcissistic Personality Disorder, providing you with a comprehensive understanding of this complex disorder.

Throughout the book, we will unravel the intricate dynamics of narcissistic abuse, helping you recognize the warning signs, manipulation tactics, and emotional impact it can have.

You will discover powerful strategies for setting and enforcing boundaries, communicating effectively with a narcissist, and reclaiming your sense of self-worth and personal power.

This book is not just about understanding narcissism; it is about reclaiming your life and finding healing after narcissistic abuse.

We will guide you through the process of healing, offering insights into self-care practices, emotional recovery, rebuilding self-esteem, and fostering healthy relationships.

Additionally, we will address the unique challenges of parenting after narcissistic abuse and provide resources and support for your ongoing journey of growth and empowerment.

Please note that the information presented in this book is meticulously researched and written by professionals in the field of psychology.

While this book provides valuable guidance, it is important to seek personalized professional help for formal diagnoses and tailored therapeutic interventions related to narcissism and Narcissistic Personality Disorder.

Importance of understanding narcissism and its impact on relationships.

Welcome to the transformative journey of unmasking narcissism and discovering empowering strategies to navigate and heal from the devastating effects of narcissistic abuse.

In this chapter, we delve into the critical importance of understanding narcissism and its profound impact on relationships, shedding light on lesser-known aspects that will empower and enlighten you.

Narcissism, a complex and intriguing psychological concept, holds significant relevance in today's world.

By exploring the depths of narcissism, we uncover the hidden layers of this personality trait, transcending the superficial stereotypes often associated with it.

Understanding narcissism goes beyond the surface-level notion of self-centeredness; it encompasses a spectrum of behaviors and traits that can range from subtle to extreme.

Recognizing the impact of narcissism on relationships is paramount to navigating the intricate dynamics that unfold within them.

Whether it is a romantic partnership, a familial connection, or a professional interaction, the presence of narcissistic traits can have far-reaching consequences.

The manipulative tactics employed by narcissists, such as gaslighting, projection, and triangulation, erode the foundations of trust, communication, and mutual respect.

Moreover, the emotional toll of narcissistic abuse is profound and often underestimated.

Victims of narcissistic abuse frequently experience anxiety, depression, low self-esteem, and a distorted sense of reality.

The insidious nature of this abuse leaves individuals questioning their own worth, sanity, and ability to trust others.

By comprehending the intricacies of narcissistic abuse, we can empower survivors to reclaim their lives, restore their self-esteem, and establish healthy boundaries.

In our exploration of narcissism, we delve into the lesser-known nuances that shape this personality trait.

We uncover the distinct subtypes of narcissism, ranging from the overt grandiose narcissist to the covert manipulator who hides behind a facade of false humility.

By unraveling these subtleties, we gain a more comprehensive understanding of the diverse manifestations of narcissism, equipping us with valuable insights for navigating these complex relationships.

While this book provides valuable knowledge and strategies, it is essential to consult with qualified professionals for personalized advice, diagnosis, and tailored therapeutic interventions related to narcissism and its impact on relationships.

Prepare yourself for a journey of self-discovery, empowerment, and healing as we embark on this exploration of unmasking narcissism and uncovering empowering strategies to navigate and heal from narcissistic abuse.

Chapter 2: Understanding Narcissism

The Spectrum of Narcissism: Exploring different levels of narcissistic traits and behaviors.

Welcome to the enlightening journey of understanding narcissism and its multifaceted nature.

In this chapter, we delve into the intricate spectrum of narcissism, exploring the diverse levels of narcissistic traits and behaviors that shape this intriguing personality trait.

Prepare to embark on a comprehensive exploration that will broaden your understanding and provide unique insights into this complex phenomenon.

Narcissism exists along a spectrum, encompassing a range of behaviors and characteristics.

At one end, we find individuals with healthy self-esteem and a balanced sense of self-worth.

Moving along the spectrum, we encounter individuals with narcissistic traits, characterized by an inflated sense of self-importance and a craving for admiration.

These individuals may exhibit self-centered tendencies and a lack of empathy, yet their behavior remains within the realm of manageable and relatively harmless.

However, as we progress further along the spectrum, we encounter individuals with Narcissistic Personality Disorder (NPD), where the traits and behaviors become more extreme and disruptive.

Those with NPD exhibit a pervasive pattern of grandiosity, a deep-seated need for constant admiration, and a lack of empathy that can have significant repercussions on their relationships and the well-being of those around them.

It is crucial to recognize that the spectrum of narcissism is not a linear scale but rather a complex interplay of various factors.

Different individuals may display distinct combinations of narcissistic traits, making the manifestations of narcissism diverse and often perplexing.

Some individuals may exhibit overt narcissism, showcasing their grandiosity and entitlement openly, while others may employ covert tactics, masking their narcissistic tendencies behind a facade of false humility and victimhood.

By understanding the intricate spectrum of narcissism, we gain valuable insights into the motives, thought patterns, and behaviors that drive individuals along this continuum.

This knowledge allows us to navigate the complexities of narcissistic relationships with heightened awareness, empowering us to establish healthy boundaries, protect our well-being, and make informed decisions regarding our interactions with narcissistic individuals.

It is important to note that the information presented in this chapter is based on extensive research, professional expertise, and real-life experiences.

While this book provides comprehensive knowledge and strategies, it is always recommended to seek personalized advice from qualified professionals for a formal diagnosis, therapeutic interventions, and tailored guidance specific to your situation.

Prepare yourself for a captivating exploration as we unravel the spectrum of narcissism, gaining a deeper understanding of its nuances and implications.

The journey ahead will equip you with powerful tools and insights to navigate the complexities of narcissistic relationships and empower you to embark on a path of healing and growth.

The DSM-5 Criteria: Examining the diagnostic criteria for Narcissistic Personality Disorder.

Welcome to an enlightening exploration of narcissism and its intricate nature.

In this chapter, we delve into the Diagnostic and Statistical Manual of Mental Disorders (DSM-5) criteria for Narcissistic Personality Disorder (NPD), unraveling the diagnostic framework and shedding light on lesser-known aspects of this complex disorder.

Get ready to dive deep into the diagnostic criteria and gain a comprehensive understanding of NPD.

The DSM-5 provides a standardized classification system used by mental health professionals to diagnose various mental disorders, including Narcissistic Personality Disorder.

To meet the criteria for NPD, an individual must exhibit a pervasive pattern of grandiosity, an insatiable need for admiration, and a lack of empathy that begins in early adulthood and manifests in a variety of contexts.

The diagnostic criteria for NPD encompass nine distinct features, and an individual must meet at least five of these to receive a formal diagnosis.

These features include a grandiose sense of self-importance, a preoccupation with fantasies of unlimited success and power, a belief in one's uniqueness and superiority, a constant need for excessive admiration, a sense of entitlement, a tendency to exploit others for personal gain, a lack of empathy, envy or the belief that others are envious of them, and arrogant and haughty behaviors or attitudes.

It is essential to note that diagnosing Narcissistic Personality Disorder requires a comprehensive assessment conducted by a qualified mental health professional.

The DSM-5 criteria serve as a valuable guideline, but a thorough evaluation of the individual's behavior, history, and overall functioning is necessary to make an accurate diagnosis.

Understanding the diagnostic criteria for NPD enables us to grasp the complexity of this disorder and its impact on individuals and their relationships.

It provides a framework for identifying and recognizing narcissistic traits and behaviors, both in ourselves and in others.

By familiarizing ourselves with these criteria, we gain the ability to discern the presence of narcissistic patterns, allowing us to navigate relationships with heightened awareness and make informed decisions about our well-being.

It is important to emphasize that the information presented in this chapter is based on reputable sources, including the DSM-5, and professional expertise in the field of psychology.

While this book provides valuable insights and strategies, it is essential to consult with qualified professionals for personalized advice, diagnosis, and tailored therapeutic interventions related to narcissism and Narcissistic Personality Disorder.

Prepare yourself for an in-depth exploration of narcissism as we continue to unmask its complexities and empower you with strategies to navigate and heal from narcissistic abuse.

The knowledge gained from understanding the diagnostic criteria for NPD will serve as a cornerstone in your journey towards reclaiming your life, fostering healthy relationships, and embarking on a path of healing and personal growth.

Subtypes of Narcissism: Investigating covert, grandiose, communal, and malignant narcissism.

Welcome to an intriguing exploration of narcissism, where we dive into the multifaceted world of different narcissistic subtypes.

In this chapter, we will investigate covert, grandiose, communal, and malignant narcissism, unraveling the distinct characteristics and behaviors that define each subtype.

Prepare yourself for a deep dive into the lesser-known aspects of narcissism that will expand your understanding and provide unique insights.

Covert Narcissism: While grandiose narcissism often grabs the spotlight, covert narcissism operates in a more subtle manner.

Covert narcissists tend to present themselves as sensitive, selfless individuals, but beneath their seemingly humble exterior lies a deep-seated need for validation and admiration.

They manipulate through passive-aggressive behaviors, playing the victim and using guilt to control others.

Grandiose Narcissism: This subtype of narcissism is perhaps the most commonly recognized.

Grandiose narcissists exude an air of superiority and entitlement, displaying an exaggerated sense of self-importance.

They seek constant admiration and validation, and their fragile self-esteem depends on external praise.

Grandiose narcissists often exploit others to fulfill their own needs and have difficulty empathizing with others.

Communal Narcissism: Unlike the traditional narcissistic archetype, communal narcissists present themselves as selfless individuals dedicated to serving others.

They derive their sense of self-worth from being seen as the ultimate caretakers or moral authorities.

However, their altruistic acts are often driven by a need for admiration and validation.

Communal narcissists may use their apparent selflessness to control and manipulate those around them.

Malignant Narcissism: This subtype represents the most extreme and dangerous manifestation of narcissism.

Malignant narcissists combine traits of grandiose narcissism with antisocial behavior and a sadistic streak.

They derive pleasure from inflicting harm on others and may display traits associated with psychopathy.

Malignant narcissists have little to no empathy and are driven by a relentless desire for power and control.

By exploring these different narcissistic subtypes, we gain a deeper understanding of the intricate and diverse nature of narcissism.

Recognizing these subtypes allows us to better identify narcissistic behaviors in ourselves and others, enabling us to navigate relationships with heightened awareness and protection of our well-being.

However, while this book provides valuable insights and strategies, it is important to consult with qualified professionals for personalized advice, diagnosis, and tailored therapeutic interventions related to narcissism and narcissistic abuse.

Prepare yourself for a captivating exploration as we continue to unmask the different subtypes of narcissism.

By understanding the distinct characteristics of covert, grandiose, communal, and malignant narcissism, you will be equipped with valuable knowledge and insights to navigate the complexities of narcissistic relationships and empower yourself to heal and grow.

The Development of Narcissism: Analyzing the potential factors contributing to the development of narcissistic traits.

Welcome to a thought-provoking exploration of narcissism, where we dive into the complex factors that contribute to the development of narcissistic traits.

In this chapter, we will analyze various potential influences, shedding light on lesser-known aspects of narcissism's origins and providing unique insights into its formation.

Prepare yourself for an in-depth exploration that will broaden your understanding and empower you with valuable knowledge.

The development of narcissism is influenced by a combination of genetic, environmental, and psychological factors.

While researchers continue to unravel the intricate web of influences, it is essential to note that narcissism is a multifaceted construct that defies simple explanations.

However, by examining some potential contributing factors, we can gain a deeper understanding of its origins.

Early Childhood Experiences: The formative years of a child play a crucial role in shaping their sense of self.

Narcissistic traits may develop as a result of parenting styles that are excessively permissive or authoritarian, neglectful or overly indulgent.

Inconsistent or invalidating parental behaviors can contribute to the development of a fragile self-esteem, leading to compensatory grandiosity or a desperate need for external validation.

Familial Influence: The family environment, including family dynamics and intergenerational patterns, can impact the development of narcissistic traits.

A family system that promotes competition, perfectionism, or places excessive emphasis on external achievements can foster a breeding ground for narcissism.

Furthermore, individuals who grow up with narcissistic parents may internalize their behaviors and adopt similar traits as a means of coping or seeking approval.

Cultural and Societal Factors: Cultural values and societal norms can shape individuals' perception of self-worth.

In cultures that prioritize individualism, material success, and self-promotion, narcissistic traits may be more prevalent.

Moreover, the rise of social media and the era of constant self-presentation can amplify narcissistic tendencies, as individuals seek validation and admiration through curated online personas.

Psychological Mechanisms: Narcissistic traits can also emerge as defense mechanisms to protect individuals from underlying feelings of insecurity, shame, or vulnerability.

By projecting an image of superiority and invulnerability, individuals with narcissistic traits shield themselves from potential emotional threats.

This defensive stance often masks deep-rooted insecurities and a fragile self-esteem.

It is important to note that the development of narcissism is a complex and nuanced process, influenced by multiple factors interacting in unique ways for each individual.

While understanding the potential factors contributing to the development of narcissistic traits is valuable, it is equally important to approach the topic with empathy and without stigmatization.

Narcissism is a spectrum, and individuals exhibiting narcissistic traits can vary significantly in their level of awareness, willingness to change, and capacity for growth.

As we delve deeper into the understanding of narcissism, we equip ourselves with valuable knowledge to navigate narcissistic relationships and empower ourselves to heal and grow.

By unraveling the potential factors that contribute to the development of narcissistic traits, we gain insights into the origins of this complex phenomenon, fostering empathy and providing a foundation for effective strategies to navigate and heal from narcissistic abuse.

Chapter 3: Identifying Narcissistic Abuse

Recognizing the Signs: Identifying the red flags and warning signs of narcissistic abuse.

Welcome to an illuminating chapter where we explore the crucial task of identifying narcissistic abuse.

In this chapter, we will delve into the intricate web of red flags and warning signs that indicate the presence of narcissistic abuse.

By recognizing these signs, you will gain valuable insights to protect yourself and others from the detrimental effects of narcissistic manipulation.

Prepare yourself for a detailed exploration that will empower you with knowledge and enable you to navigate the challenging terrain of narcissistic relationships.

Identifying narcissistic abuse requires a keen understanding of the tactics employed by narcissists to exert control and manipulate their victims.

While each situation may vary, there are common patterns and behaviors that serve as warning signs.

By familiarizing yourself with these signs, you will be equipped with the tools to identify and address narcissistic abuse effectively.

Emotional Manipulation: Narcissists excel at manipulating emotions and exploiting vulnerabilities.

They may employ tactics such as gaslighting, where they distort your perception of reality and make you doubt your own sanity.

They may also engage in constant criticism, belittling, or undermining your self-esteem to maintain control and dominance.

Lack of Empathy: One of the defining characteristics of narcissistic abuse is the absence of genuine empathy from the abuser.

They are unable or unwilling to understand or relate to your emotions, dismissing or minimizing your feelings.

They may also lack remorse for their hurtful actions, shifting blame onto you or others.

Control and Domination: Narcissistic abusers strive for power and control over their victims.

They may employ various tactics to achieve this, including isolating you from friends and family, monitoring your activities, and dictating your behavior.

They may also engage in financial, sexual, or psychological manipulation to maintain dominance.

Triangulation and Devaluation: Narcissists often create a dynamic of competition and comparison by triangulating you with other individuals.

They may praise one person while devaluing you, instilling insecurity and fostering dependency.

This tactic serves to reinforce their control and maintain their power over you.

It is important to note that narcissistic abuse can occur in various types of relationships, including romantic partnerships, family dynamics, friendships, or professional settings.

It transcends gender, age, and cultural boundaries, making it crucial to be vigilant and aware of the signs in all aspects of life.

By understanding the red flags and warning signs of narcissistic abuse, you gain the ability to identify unhealthy dynamics and make informed decisions about your relationships.

Remember, seeking support from qualified professionals, such as therapists or counselors specializing in narcissistic abuse, can provide invaluable guidance and assistance in navigating the complexities of healing and recovery.

Prepare yourself for a transformative journey as we continue to unravel the strategies and empower you with effective tools to navigate and heal from narcissistic abuse.

By identifying the signs of narcissistic abuse, you are taking an essential step towards reclaiming your life and fostering healthy relationships built on mutual respect and genuine connection.

Emotional Manipulation Techniques: Understanding gaslighting, projection, blame-shifting, and other manipulation tactics employed by narcissists.

Welcome to an enlightening chapter where we delve into the intricate world of narcissistic abuse and explore the emotional manipulation techniques employed by narcissists.

In this chapter, we will unravel the tactics of gaslighting, projection, blame-shifting, and other manipulation strategies utilized by narcissists to exert control and dominance over their victims.

By understanding these techniques, you will gain valuable insights to identify and combat emotional manipulation, empowering you to navigate the complex terrain of narcissistic relationships.

Gaslighting: is a pervasive form of emotional manipulation used by narcissists to distort your perception of reality.

Through subtle and consistent tactics, they undermine your confidence in your own thoughts, feelings, and experiences.

Gaslighting often involves invalidating your emotions, denying past events, or even making you question your own sanity.

By sowing seeds of doubt and confusion, narcissists gain control and power over you.

Projection: is another manipulation technique commonly employed by narcissists.

They project their own undesirable traits, feelings, and behaviors onto their victims.

By deflecting accountability and blaming you for their actions, they avoid taking responsibility for their own shortcomings.

This tactic serves to maintain their self-image of superiority and to shift the focus away from their own flaws.

Blame-shifting: is yet another manipulation strategy used by narcissists to avoid accountability.

They deflect blame onto others, including their victims, and refuse to acknowledge their own role in conflicts or negative situations.

By shifting the blame, they protect their fragile self-esteem and preserve their image of faultlessness.

This tactic can leave victims feeling confused, guilty, and responsible for problems that are not theirs to bear.

In addition to gaslighting, projection, and blame-shifting, narcissists may employ a range of other manipulation techniques to control and dominate their victims.

These tactics include manipulation through guilt, love bombing (excessive affection and attention followed by withdrawal), triangulation (creating competition and jealousy), and silent treatment (ignoring or withdrawing emotional presence).

It is important to note that emotional manipulation techniques can vary in intensity and frequency depending on the individual narcissist.

Furthermore, not all narcissists may employ every tactic listed.

However, by familiarizing yourself with these manipulation techniques, you will gain a deeper understanding of the dynamics at play and be better equipped to identify and address emotional manipulation in your relationships.

By recognizing the emotional manipulation techniques utilized by narcissists, you empower yourself to protect your emotional well-being and regain control over your life.

Remember, healing from narcissistic abuse requires support and guidance from qualified professionals who specialize in this area.

Therapists, counselors, and support groups can provide invaluable assistance as you navigate the complexities of healing and recovery.

By equipping yourself with knowledge and seeking the support you need, you take an important step toward reclaiming your power and building a future free from the grip of narcissistic abuse.

Prepare yourself for the transformative journey ahead as we continue to explore empowering strategies to navigate and heal from narcissistic abuse.

By understanding the emotional manipulation techniques employed by narcissists, you gain the ability to recognize these patterns and protect yourself from their harmful effects.

Reclaim your power, rebuild your self-esteem, and foster healthy, fulfilling relationships founded on mutual respect and genuine connection.

Triangulation and Smear Campaigns: Exploring how narcissists use triangulation and smear campaigns to control and isolate their victims.

Welcome to an insightful chapter where we delve into the complex dynamics of narcissistic abuse and explore the insidious tactics of triangulation and smear campaigns employed by narcissists.

In this chapter, we will uncover the manipulative strategies used by narcissists to control, isolate, and undermine their victims through the use of triangulation and smear campaigns.

By understanding these tactics, you will gain valuable insights to identify and combat the detrimental effects of narcissistic abuse, empowering you to navigate the challenging terrain of these toxic relationships.

Triangulation: is a psychological tactic used by narcissists to create a dynamic of competition and comparison between their victims and others.

By involving a third party, the narcissist instills feelings of insecurity, jealousy, and inadequacy within the victim.

They may compare the victim to the third party, praising the third party's achievements or positive qualities while simultaneously devaluing and belittling the victim.

This manipulation tactic serves to reinforce the narcissist's control over the victim and maintain a power imbalance within the relationship.

Smear campaigns: are another weapon utilized by narcissists to tarnish the reputation and credibility of their victims.

In a smear campaign, the narcissist spreads false information, rumors, or distorted narratives about the victim to others, including friends, family, colleagues, and community members.

This calculated effort aims to isolate the victim by turning people against them, eroding their support system, and creating a sense of social ostracism.

The narcissist may employ tactics such as character assassination, gaslighting, and manipulation to ensure the success of their smear campaign.

It is important to note that both triangulation and smear campaigns are deliberate strategies employed by narcissists to assert control and dominance over their victims.

They exploit the victim's vulnerabilities and emotions to create chaos and confusion, leaving the victim feeling isolated, invalidated, and powerless.

By understanding these tactics, you will be better equipped to recognize the signs of narcissistic abuse and take steps to protect yourself.

By shedding light on the manipulative tactics of triangulation and smear campaigns, we aim to empower individuals who have experienced narcissistic abuse to reclaim their sense of self and break free from the destructive cycle.

Remember, healing from narcissistic abuse requires support and guidance from qualified professionals who specialize in this area.

Therapists, counselors, and support groups can provide invaluable assistance as you navigate the complexities of healing and recovery.

By equipping yourself with knowledge and seeking the support you need, you take an important step toward breaking free from the control of narcissistic abuse and rebuilding a life of strength, resilience, and self-worth.

Prepare yourself for the transformative journey ahead as we continue to explore empowering strategies to navigate and heal from narcissistic abuse.

By understanding the tactics of triangulation and smear campaigns, you gain the ability to recognize and counteract these manipulative efforts, protecting your emotional well-being and regaining control over your life.

Reclaim your power, restore your sense of self, and forge healthy, authentic connections built on trust and mutual respect.

Covert Narcissism: Uncovering the hidden abuse of covert narcissists.

Welcome to an illuminating chapter where we delve into the intricate world of narcissistic abuse and shine a spotlight on the hidden abuse of covert narcissists.

In this chapter, we will uncover the distinct characteristics and tactics employed by covert narcissists, providing you with valuable insights to identify and navigate the complexities of covert narcissistic abuse.

By understanding the subtle nature of covert narcissism, you will gain the knowledge and tools to protect yourself and embark on a journey of healing and empowerment.

Covert narcissism, also known as vulnerable narcissism or shy narcissism, is a subtype of narcissistic personality disorder (NPD) that differs from the more overt and grandiose form commonly associated with narcissism.

While overt narcissists display their arrogance and sense of superiority openly, covert narcissists hide their narcissistic tendencies beneath a veneer of humility, victimhood, or excessive sensitivity.

Their abuse is often insidious and covert, making it challenging to detect and confront.

One of the key characteristics of covert narcissists is their profound need for validation and admiration, which they may seek through a facade of modesty and selflessness.

They may present themselves as self-sacrificing, caring individuals who put others' needs before their own.

However, beneath this mask of apparent empathy lies a deep sense of entitlement and a constant need for admiration and validation from others.

Covert narcissists are skilled manipulators who exploit the empathy and compassion of their victims, using subtle tactics to gain control and exert power.

Unlike their overt counterparts, covert narcissists are adept at playing the victim.

They may use emotional manipulation techniques, such as guilt-tripping, to manipulate others into meeting their needs and maintaining control.

They often employ passive-aggressive behaviors, withholding affection or attention as a means of punishment or control.

Covert narcissists excel at deflecting responsibility, shifting blame onto others, and evading accountability for their actions.

Their abuse is often characterized by a pattern of subtle manipulation, emotional invalidation, and gaslighting, leaving their victims feeling confused, invalidated, and responsible for the dysfunction in the relationship.

It is crucial to recognize the nuances of covert narcissism to protect yourself from its harmful effects.

By understanding the distinct characteristics and tactics employed by covert narcissists, you can begin to identify the subtle signs of abuse and develop strategies to navigate these challenging relationships.

However, it is important to approach the identification and management of covert narcissistic abuse with the guidance and support of qualified professionals who specialize in this area.

By shedding light on the hidden abuse of covert narcissists, we aim to empower individuals who have experienced narcissistic abuse to recognize the manipulative tactics and reclaim their power and well-being.

Remember, healing from narcissistic abuse requires a multifaceted approach that includes therapy, self-care, and a supportive network of individuals who understand and validate your experiences.

By equipping yourself with knowledge and seeking the support you need, you can break free from the grip of covert narcissistic abuse and embark on a path of healing, self-discovery, and personal growth.

Prepare yourself for the transformative journey ahead as we continue to explore empowering strategies to navigate and heal from narcissistic abuse.

By understanding the intricacies of covert narcissism, you gain the ability to recognize the subtle signs of abuse and take proactive steps towards breaking free from the cycle.

Reclaim your self-worth, establish healthy boundaries, and cultivate relationships rooted in authenticity and mutual respect.

Chapter 4: The Impact of Narcissistic Abuse

Emotional Abuse: Examining the profound emotional toll of narcissistic abuse, including anxiety, depression, and low self-esteem.

Welcome to a profound chapter where we explore the devastating impact of narcissistic abuse on one's emotional well-being.

In this chapter, we delve into the intricate web of emotional abuse inflicted by narcissists, shedding light on the profound toll it takes on individuals' mental and emotional health.

By understanding the far-reaching consequences of narcissistic abuse, including anxiety, depression, and low self-esteem, we can begin to unravel its grip and embark on a journey of healing and empowerment.

Emotional abuse within the context of narcissistic relationships is a relentless assault on one's sense of self-worth, identity, and emotional stability.

Unlike physical abuse, emotional abuse often leaves no visible scars, making it difficult for victims to recognize and validate their experiences.

Narcissists employ a wide array of manipulative tactics designed to undermine their victims' confidence, create dependency, and maintain control.

Anxiety: is a common outcome of narcissistic abuse, stemming from the constant state of hyper-vigilance and fear cultivated by the narcissist.

Victims are constantly on edge, anticipating the next verbal attack, emotional manipulation, or unpredictable behavior from the narcissist.

The gaslighting and invalidation experienced in these relationships further exacerbate anxiety symptoms, leading to heightened feelings of unease, insecurity, and uncertainty.

Depression: often accompanies the aftermath of narcissistic abuse, as victims struggle with a profound sense of loss, grief, and despair.

The relentless psychological manipulation and emotional rollercoaster imposed by the narcissist erode one's self-esteem, leaving them feeling worthless, helpless, and disconnected from their own emotions.

The prolonged exposure to such toxic dynamics can lead to a deepening sense of hopelessness, sadness, and even thoughts of self-harm or suicide.

Low self-esteem: is a pervasive consequence of narcissistic abuse, as the narcissist systematically dismantles their victim's self-worth and instills a profound sense of inadequacy.

Victims are consistently subjected to criticism, belittlement, and devaluation, eroding their confidence, autonomy, and trust in their own perceptions.

The relentless comparison to others, invalidation of their emotions, and constant need for approval from the narcissist leaves them feeling unworthy of love, respect, and happiness.

It is important to acknowledge that the impact of narcissistic abuse extends beyond the emotional realm, affecting various aspects of one's life, including relationships, work, and overall well-being.

Recognizing and addressing the emotional aftermath of narcissistic abuse is crucial for healing and recovery.

Seeking support from qualified professionals, such as therapists and counselors specializing in trauma and narcissistic abuse, is an essential step toward reclaiming your mental and emotional well-being.

Additionally, engaging in self-care practices, establishing healthy boundaries, and cultivating a support network of understanding individuals can contribute to your healing journey.

Prepare yourself for the transformative journey ahead as we continue to explore empowering strategies to navigate and heal from narcissistic abuse.

By understanding the profound emotional toll of narcissistic abuse, including anxiety, depression, and low self-esteem, you can begin to rebuild a life rooted in self-compassion, resilience, and authentic self-worth.

Reclaim your emotional freedom, rediscover your inner strength, and forge a path toward healing, growth, and empowerment.

Complex Post-Traumatic Stress Disorder (C-PTSD): Discussing the long-term consequences of narcissistic abuse, including trauma bonding and emotional flashbacks.

Welcome to a pivotal chapter where we explore the profound impact of narcissistic abuse and its long-term consequences on individuals' mental and emotional well-being.

In this chapter, we delve into the complex realm of post-traumatic stress disorder (PTSD) and its variant, complex post-traumatic stress disorder (C-PTSD), shedding light on the intricate dynamics of trauma bonding and emotional flashbacks that often accompany narcissistic abuse.

By understanding the profound and lasting effects of narcissistic abuse, we can begin to navigate our path toward healing and reclaiming our lives.

Complex post-traumatic stress disorder (C-PTSD): is a distinct form of PTSD that arises from prolonged exposure to traumatic events, such as narcissistic abuse.

While both PTSD and C-PTSD share common symptoms, such as intrusive memories, nightmares, and hypervigilance, C-PTSD encompasses a broader range of symptoms that reflect the chronic and complex nature of the trauma experienced.

One of the significant aspects of C-PTSD in the context of narcissistic abuse is trauma bonding.

Trauma bonding refers to the strong emotional attachment that forms between the victim and the abuser as a result of the alternating cycles of abuse and intermittent reinforcement.

The narcissist employs manipulative tactics such as love bombing, devaluation, and intermittent acts of kindness to create a powerful psychological bond with the victim.

This bond can make it extremely challenging for the victim to break free from the abusive relationship, as they become entangled in a complex web of conflicting emotions, dependence, and a skewed sense of loyalty.

Emotional flashbacks: are another debilitating aspect of C-PTSD experienced by survivors of narcissistic abuse.

Unlike typical flashbacks associated with PTSD, which involve vivid re-experiencing of a traumatic event, emotional flashbacks primarily involve a sudden and overwhelming resurgence of intense emotional states associated with the abuse.

These flashbacks can be triggered by certain words, behaviors, or situations that resemble past experiences of abuse.

Victims may find themselves flooded with emotions of fear, shame, anger, or helplessness, even when there is no immediate threat present.

Emotional flashbacks can disrupt daily functioning, destabilize relationships, and further reinforce the trauma bond with the narcissistic abuser.

Understanding and addressing the long-term consequences of narcissistic abuse, including C-PTSD, trauma bonding, and emotional flashbacks, is crucial for healing and recovery.

By seeking support from qualified professionals, such as therapists specializing in trauma and narcissistic abuse, survivors can gain insights, tools, and strategies to navigate the complex aftermath of abuse.

Therapeutic interventions, such as trauma-focused therapy, cognitive-behavioral therapy, and somatic experiencing, can aid in processing the trauma, rebuilding self-esteem, and developing healthy coping mechanisms.

Additionally, engaging in self-care practices, such as mindfulness, meditation, exercise, and creative outlets, can help survivors manage their emotions, reduce anxiety, and foster a sense of empowerment.

Building a strong support network of understanding individuals, participating in support groups or online communities, and educating oneself about narcissism and its effects can also provide validation, guidance, and a sense of belonging.

Prepare yourself for the transformative journey ahead as we continue to explore empowering strategies to navigate and heal from narcissistic abuse.

By recognizing the long-term consequences of narcissistic abuse, including complex post-traumatic stress disorder, trauma bonding, and emotional flashbacks, you can begin to reclaim your life, rediscover your inner strength, and forge a path toward healing, growth, and empowerment.

Break free from the chains of abuse, embrace your resilience, and embark on a journey of self-discovery and recovery.

Cognitive Dissonance: Exploring the internal struggle victims face when the narcissist's words and actions don't align.

Welcome to Chapter 4, where we delve into the profound impact of narcissistic abuse and explore the intricate psychological phenomenon known as cognitive dissonance.

In this chapter, we shed light on the internal struggle victims face when the narcissist's words and actions don't align, creating a state of confusion, self-doubt, and emotional turmoil.

By understanding cognitive dissonance and its role in narcissistic abuse, we can begin to unravel the complexities of our experiences and find empowerment in our healing journey.

Cognitive dissonance refers to the psychological discomfort that arises when there is a discrepancy between our beliefs, attitudes, or values and our behavior or the information we encounter.

In the context of narcissistic abuse, cognitive dissonance occurs when the victim experiences conflicting thoughts and emotions due to the stark contrast between the charming facade the narcissist presents and their hurtful actions behind closed doors.

This dissonance can create a state of confusion, self-blame, and a persistent hope that the narcissist will change, leading the victim to question their own perceptions and reality.

One of the reasons cognitive dissonance is prevalent in narcissistic abuse is because narcissists are masters of manipulation and deception.

They possess a charming and charismatic persona that can be difficult to reconcile with their abusive behaviors.

This creates a constant back-and-forth struggle within the victim's mind as they try to make sense of the contradiction between the narcissist's words of love and adoration and their hurtful actions of control, manipulation, and emotional abuse.

Victims of narcissistic abuse often find themselves trapped in a cycle of cognitive dissonance, desperately searching for ways to reconcile the contradiction they experience.

They may engage in rationalization, making excuses for the narcissist's behavior or blaming themselves for the abuse.

They may also engage in minimization, downplaying the severity of the abuse or denying its impact on their well-being.

This internal battle can have profound psychological and emotional consequences, leading to feelings of self-doubt, anxiety, and a diminished sense of self-worth.

To navigate the challenges of cognitive dissonance, it is crucial for victims to gain a deeper understanding of narcissism and the tactics employed by narcissists.

By educating themselves about narcissistic personality disorder and the manipulative strategies used by narcissists, victims can begin to break free from the grip of cognitive dissonance and gain clarity about their experiences.

Seeking support from trusted friends, family, or therapists who specialize in narcissistic abuse can provide validation, guidance, and a safe space to explore and process conflicting emotions.

Engaging in self-care practices, such as journaling, mindfulness, and self-reflection, can also help victims reconnect with their own inner voice and regain a sense of personal agency.

It is essential to remember that cognitive dissonance is a normal response to the contradictions inherent in narcissistic abuse.

By acknowledging and understanding this internal struggle, victims can start to untangle themselves from the web of confusion and take steps towards healing and reclaiming their lives.

As we move forward in this journey of unmasking narcissism and empowering ourselves to navigate and heal from narcissistic abuse, let us embrace the complexities of cognitive dissonance, challenge the distorted narratives imposed upon us, and strive for a future grounded in authenticity, self-compassion, and personal growth.

Financial and Legal Abuse: Shedding light on the financial and legal aspects of narcissistic abuse, such as economic control and manipulation.

Welcome to Chapter 4, where we dive into the often overlooked but impactful aspects of narcissistic abuse—financial and legal abuse.

In this chapter, we shine a light on the intricate ways in which narcissists exert control and manipulate their victims through economic means.

By understanding the dynamics of financial and legal abuse, we can equip ourselves with knowledge and strategies to navigate these challenges and regain our financial independence and personal power.

Financial abuse: is a form of control and manipulation that narcissists employ to maintain power and dominance over their victims.

It can take various forms, such as controlling the victim's access to money, withholding financial resources, or coercing the victim into financial dependency.

Narcissists may exploit joint bank accounts, run up debts in the victim's name, or sabotage the victim's financial stability to assert control and undermine their autonomy.

Victims often find themselves trapped in a web of financial constraints, unable to make independent decisions or escape the clutches of the narcissist.

Legal abuse: is another insidious tactic used by narcissists to further exert control and intimidate their victims.

They may engage in frivolous lawsuits, file false accusations, or manipulate the legal system to intimidate and exhaust their victims emotionally and financially.

By weaponizing the legal system, narcissists aim to instill fear, create confusion, and maintain their power and control over the victim's life.

To navigate the complexities of financial and legal abuse, it is crucial to seek professional help and guidance.

Consulting with an attorney who specializes in domestic abuse and family law can provide valuable insights and support in understanding your rights and legal options.

They can assist in developing strategies to protect your assets, secure financial independence, and navigate the legal proceedings with confidence.

Financial empowerment is a key aspect of healing from narcissistic abuse.

Taking steps to regain control of your finances can be liberating and help you rebuild your life.

This may involve creating a separate bank account, establishing a budget, and seeking financial counseling to develop a solid financial plan.

Educating yourself about personal finance, investments, and building financial resilience can be empowering and enable you to take charge of your financial future.

In addition to professional assistance, it is essential to surround yourself with a strong support system.

Reach out to friends, family, or support groups who understand the complexities of narcissistic abuse and can provide emotional support, guidance, and encouragement.

Together, you can share experiences, resources, and strategies for overcoming the financial and legal challenges posed by narcissistic abuse.

As we continue our journey of unmasking narcissism and empowering ourselves to navigate and heal from narcissistic abuse, let us shine a light on the often hidden aspects of financial and legal abuse.

By arming ourselves with knowledge, seeking professional help, and building a strong support network, we can break free from the shackles of financial and legal control, reclaim our autonomy, and move towards a future filled with financial security and personal empowerment.

Chapter 5: Establishing Boundaries

The Importance of Boundaries: Understanding why boundaries are crucial in dealing with narcissists.

Welcome to Chapter 5, where we delve into the critical topic of establishing boundaries when dealing with narcissists.

In this chapter, we explore the significance of boundaries and why they are crucial in navigating and healing from narcissistic abuse.

By understanding the importance of boundaries and learning effective strategies to establish and maintain them, we can regain control over our lives and protect ourselves from further harm.

Boundaries: serve as a protective shield against the manipulative tactics of narcissists.

They define what is acceptable and unacceptable behavior, establish limits on how others can treat us, and safeguard our emotional and physical well-being.

For individuals who have experienced narcissistic abuse, setting boundaries is an essential step in reclaiming their power, rebuilding self-esteem, and creating a healthier and more balanced life.

When dealing with narcissists, it is crucial to recognize that they have a relentless need for control and dominance.

They often push boundaries, disregard personal boundaries, and exploit any perceived weaknesses or vulnerabilities.

By understanding this dynamic, we can begin to assert our own boundaries and protect ourselves from further manipulation and abuse.

Establishing boundaries requires self-reflection and self-awareness.

It involves understanding our own needs, values, and limits.

By identifying what is important to us and what we will no longer tolerate, we can begin to set clear and firm boundaries.

This process may involve examining past experiences, recognizing patterns of abuse, and identifying the specific behaviors or actions that are detrimental to our well-being.

Effective boundary-setting also requires effective communication.

It is essential to express our boundaries assertively and confidently, without aggression or hostility.

Clearly and calmly communicate our limits, expectations, and consequences for crossing those boundaries.

By doing so, we establish a clear message that our well-being is non-negotiable and that we will not tolerate further abuse or manipulation.

It is important to anticipate that narcissists may react negatively to our boundaries.

They may challenge, dismiss, or attempt to undermine them.

It is crucial to stand firm and maintain consistency in enforcing our boundaries.

Remember, establishing boundaries is about protecting ourselves and reclaiming our power, not about seeking validation or approval from the narcissist.

Building a support network of trusted individuals who understand and respect our boundaries is essential.

Surrounding ourselves with people who support and reinforce our boundaries can provide a sense of validation and encouragement.

They can offer guidance, empathy, and strength during challenging times and help us maintain our commitment to our boundaries.

As we embark on the journey of establishing boundaries, it is important to remember that it is a process.

It may take time, practice, and adjustment to find the right balance that works for us.

Be patient with yourself and celebrate each step forward, no matter how small.

By establishing and maintaining healthy boundaries, we reclaim our personal power, protect our well-being, and pave the way for healing and growth.

In Chapter 5, we have explored the importance of boundaries in dealing with narcissists.

By understanding their significance, recognizing our own needs and limits, and effectively communicating and enforcing boundaries, we can regain control over our lives and establish healthier relationships.

Join us as we continue to navigate the path of unmasking narcissism and empowering ourselves to heal and thrive.

Identifying Personal Boundaries and Values: Helping readers define their personal boundaries and values to establish a solid foundation.

Welcome to Chapter 5, where we embark on the journey of establishing boundaries as a crucial step in navigating and healing from narcissistic abuse.

In this chapter, we delve into the process of identifying personal boundaries and values to establish a solid foundation for reclaiming our power and creating healthier relationships.

By gaining clarity on our boundaries and aligning them with our core values, we can establish a strong framework that guides our interactions and protects our well-being.

To begin, let's explore the concept of personal boundaries.

Personal boundaries are the invisible lines that define the limits of what is acceptable and unacceptable in our relationships and interactions with others.

They act as a safeguard for our emotional, mental, and physical well-being, ensuring that we are treated with respect and dignity.

Identifying our personal boundaries requires deep self-reflection and introspection.

It involves examining our thoughts, emotions, and experiences to determine what feels comfortable and what crosses the line into discomfort or violation.

Reflecting on past experiences of narcissistic abuse can provide valuable insights into areas where our boundaries have been compromised or violated.

In addition to identifying boundaries, it is equally important to clarify our core values.

Our values are the guiding principles that shape our behavior, decisions, and priorities.

They reflect what is most important to us and define our sense of integrity and authenticity.

By aligning our boundaries with our core values, we create a solid foundation rooted in self-respect and self-care.

When identifying personal boundaries and values, it can be helpful to ask ourselves thought-provoking questions such as:

- What behaviors do I find unacceptable?
- What are my non-negotiables in relationships?
- How do I want to be treated by others?
- What values are most important to me?

Taking the time to explore these questions allows us to gain clarity and establish a clear roadmap for setting boundaries.

As we uncover our personal boundaries and values, it is essential to honor and respect them.

This requires assertive communication and boundary enforcement.

Assertive communication involves expressing our needs, desires, and limits in a clear, direct, and respectful manner.

It empowers us to advocate for ourselves and assert our boundaries without aggression or passivity.

Enforcing our boundaries involves setting consequences for those who repeatedly violate them.

It requires consistency and the willingness to prioritize our well-being over the discomfort of others.

It's important to remember that boundaries are not meant to be punitive but rather protective.

By enforcing our boundaries, we send a clear message that we deserve to be treated with respect and that our boundaries are non-negotiable.

Establishing and maintaining personal boundaries is an ongoing process that requires self-awareness, self-care, and continuous evaluation.

As we grow and evolve, our boundaries may shift and adapt. It's essential to regularly reassess our boundaries and ensure they align with our evolving needs and values.

In Chapter 5, we have explored the crucial task of identifying personal boundaries and values.

By gaining clarity on our boundaries and aligning them with our core values, we establish a strong foundation for healthy relationships and self-empowerment.

Join us as we continue our journey of unmasking narcissism and empowering ourselves to navigate and heal from narcissistic abuse.

Communicating Boundaries: Strategies for effectively communicating boundaries to narcissists while maintaining personal safety.

Welcome to Chapter 5, where we delve into the crucial task of establishing boundaries in the face of narcissistic abuse.

In this chapter, we explore the art of communicating boundaries effectively to narcissists while prioritizing personal safety.

Communicating boundaries to narcissists requires a unique approach due to their manipulative and self-centered nature.

By employing specific strategies and techniques, we can assert our boundaries while minimizing the risk of escalating abuse.

One of the fundamental strategies for communicating boundaries to narcissists is maintaining a calm and composed demeanor.

Narcissists thrive on conflict and drama, and they often use emotional reactions as a means to undermine and control their victims.

By remaining composed and emotionally detached, we deprive them of the ammunition they seek.

It's important to remember that our emotions are valid, but expressing them in a controlled manner can be more effective in getting our message across.

Another strategy is to use assertive communication techniques when communicating our boundaries.

Assertive communication: involves expressing our needs, wants, and limits in a clear, direct, and respectful manner.

It's important to use "I" statements to emphasize personal boundaries and avoid blaming or accusing language.

For example, instead of saying, "You always make me feel small," we can say, "I need to be treated with respect and consideration."

When communicating boundaries to narcissists, it's crucial to anticipate and prepare for potential pushback or manipulation.

Narcissists are skilled at twisting words, gaslighting, and manipulating situations to maintain control.

Therefore, it can be helpful to practice our responses in advance, envision different scenarios, and develop assertive yet firm responses that protect our boundaries.

By being prepared, we can minimize the likelihood of being caught off guard or manipulated into compromising our boundaries.

Additionally, it's important to set consequences for boundary violations and enforce them consistently.

Narcissists often test boundaries to see if we are serious about enforcing them.

By setting clear consequences and following through with them, we establish a sense of accountability and demonstrate that our boundaries are non-negotiable.

Consequences may include limiting contact, setting boundaries around specific topics, or seeking support from trusted individuals or professionals.

Maintaining personal safety is of utmost importance when communicating boundaries to narcissists.

If we feel physically threatened or in immediate danger, it's crucial to prioritize our well-being and seek help from authorities or domestic violence hotlines.

Safety planning, which involves identifying safe spaces and developing an exit strategy if necessary, can be essential for those in high-risk situations.

In Chapter 5, we have explored strategies for effectively communicating boundaries to narcissists while ensuring personal safety.

By maintaining a calm demeanour, using assertive communication techniques, preparing for potential manipulation, setting consequences, and prioritizing personal safety, we empower ourselves to navigate the complexities of narcissistic abuse.

Join us as we continue our journey of unmasking narcissism and discovering empowering strategies to navigate and heal from narcissistic abuse.

Enforcing Boundaries: Exploring techniques for enforcing boundaries and dealing with the narcissist's response.

Welcome to Chapter 5, where we delve into the crucial task of establishing boundaries in the face of narcissistic abuse.

In this chapter, we explore empowering techniques for enforcing boundaries and navigate the often challenging responses from narcissists.

Enforcing boundaries: with narcissists can be a complex and delicate process, but with the right strategies, we can assert our limits and protect our well-being.

One effective technique for enforcing boundaries is maintaining consistency.

Narcissists often test boundaries to gauge our resolve and willingness to enforce them.

By consistently upholding our boundaries and not wavering in our stance, we send a clear message that our limits are non-negotiable.

This requires a firm and unwavering commitment to ourselves and our well-being.

Another important aspect of enforcing boundaries is practicing self-care.

Narcissists may respond to boundary enforcement with manipulation, guilt-tripping, or attempts to undermine our confidence.

It's crucial to prioritize self-care during these interactions.

Taking care of our physical and emotional well-being through activities like exercise, meditation, therapy, and spending time with supportive loved ones can help us stay grounded and resilient.

It's also essential to practice assertiveness when dealing with the narcissist's response to our boundaries.

Narcissists may resort to gaslighting, blame-shifting, or other manipulative tactics to undermine our boundaries.

By maintaining a confident and assertive tone, we assert our rights and make it clear that we will not tolerate their attempts to manipulate or control us.

Remember, assertiveness is not aggression or confrontation; it is a firm yet respectful communication style that allows us to protect our boundaries.

Setting consequences for boundary violations is another powerful technique.

Narcissists often push boundaries to test our resolve.

By establishing clear consequences for their actions and following through with them, we establish a sense of accountability.

Consequences may include limiting contact, setting boundaries around specific topics, or seeking professional intervention.

By enforcing consequences, we communicate that our boundaries are not negotiable.

Navigating the response of a narcissist when enforcing boundaries can be challenging, and it's essential to be prepared for potential resistance.

They may escalate their manipulative tactics, attempt to guilt-trip or discredit us, or even resort to anger or aggression.

It's important to remain firm, composed, and seek support from trusted friends, family, or professionals who understand the dynamics of narcissistic abuse.

In Chapter 5, we have explored techniques for enforcing boundaries and navigating the responses of narcissists.

By maintaining consistency, practicing self-care, being assertive, setting consequences, and seeking support, we empower ourselves to establish and uphold our boundaries in the face of narcissistic abuse.

Join us as we continue our journey of unmasking narcissism and discovering empowering strategies to navigate and heal from narcissistic abuse.

Chapter 6: Communicating Effectively with a Narcissist

Assertive Communication: Teaching assertiveness techniques to maintain self-respect and communicate needs effectively.

Welcome to Chapter 6, where we explore the art of communicating effectively with a narcissist.

In this chapter, we dive into assertive communication techniques that can help maintain our self-respect while effectively conveying our needs to the narcissist.

Communicating with a narcissist can be a daunting task, given their tendencies towards defensiveness, manipulation, and self-centeredness.

However, with the right strategies, we can navigate these challenges and assert ourselves with confidence.

One key aspect of communicating with a narcissist is practicing assertiveness.

Assertive communication: involves expressing our thoughts, feelings, and needs in a clear, confident, and respectful manner.

It allows us to stand up for ourselves while maintaining a healthy level of self-respect.

When communicating with a narcissist, it's crucial to use "I" statements to express our perspective and avoid blaming or attacking language.

This approach helps minimize their defensiveness and increases the chances of being heard.

Active listening is another vital component of effective communication.

Narcissists often crave attention and validation, so actively listening to their concerns and acknowledging their perspective can help create a more conducive environment for communication.

However, it's important to maintain boundaries and not get entangled in their manipulative tactics or fall prey to their gaslighting attempts.

Active listening should be balanced with discernment and a focus on our own well-being.

Setting realistic expectations is essential when communicating with a narcissist.

It's crucial to understand that narcissists are unlikely to change their fundamental behaviors or perspectives.

Therefore, we should adjust our expectations and focus on protecting our own boundaries and well-being.

This means being clear about our own needs and limitations and not expecting the narcissist to fulfill them.

By setting realistic expectations, we can reduce frustration and disappointment in our interactions with the narcissist.

Another effective technique in communicating with a narcissist is choosing the right timing and environment.

Selecting a neutral and calm setting can help minimize potential triggers and defensiveness.

It's advisable to avoid confrontations or discussions when the narcissist is in an agitated state or during times of high stress.

By choosing the right timing and environment, we increase the chances of having a more productive and less confrontational conversation.

In Chapter 6, we have explored assertive communication techniques for effectively engaging with a narcissist.

By practicing assertiveness, active listening, setting realistic expectations, and choosing the right timing and environment, we empower ourselves to communicate our needs while maintaining self-respect.

Join us as we continue our journey of unmasking narcissism and discovering empowering strategies to navigate and heal from narcissistic abuse.

Gray Rock Method: Introducing the Gray Rock method as a means of minimizing the narcissist's ability to provoke and manipulate.

In Chapter 6, we delve into the fascinating world of effective communication with a narcissist and introduce you to a powerful strategy known as the Gray Rock method.

When dealing with a narcissist, it can feel like walking on a tightrope, as they thrive on attention and can easily provoke and manipulate those around them.

However, the Gray Rock method offers a way to minimize their ability to affect us emotionally and disrupt our lives.

The Gray Rock: method involves adopting a neutral and uninteresting demeanor when interacting with a narcissist.

It is based on the concept of becoming as unremarkable and unresponsive as a gray rock, rendering ourselves uninteresting to the narcissist.

By doing so, we reduce their desire to engage us and drain our emotional energy.

The key to successfully implementing the Gray Rock method lies in mastering the art of emotional detachment.

It requires us to maintain a calm and composed demeanor, even in the face of their provocations or manipulations.

This means avoiding emotional reactions, not feeding into their attempts to provoke us, and steering clear of engaging in arguments or power struggles.

Instead, we become observers, detached from their attempts to control or manipulate us.

One of the advantages of the Gray Rock method is that it gradually diminishes the narcissist's interest in us.

By providing them with little emotional feedback or gratification, we become less appealing as targets for their manipulation.

However, it is important to note that implementing this method requires careful planning and consideration for personal safety.

If the narcissist becomes aware of our change in behavior, they may intensify their efforts to regain control.

Therefore, it's crucial to have support systems in place and seek professional guidance if necessary.

The Gray Rock method is not a magical solution that will instantly transform the dynamics of our relationship with a narcissist.

However, when combined with other empowering strategies, such as establishing boundaries and practicing self-care, it can be a valuable tool in minimizing the impact of their manipulations and maintaining our emotional well-being.

In Chapter 6, we have explored the Gray Rock method as a means of reducing the narcissist's ability to provoke and manipulate.

By adopting a neutral and uninteresting demeanor, practicing emotional detachment, and seeking support, we can regain control over our interactions with a narcissist.

Join us as we continue our journey of unmasking narcissism and discovering empowering strategies to navigate and heal from narcissistic abuse.

Setting Realistic Expectations: Managing expectations when engaging in communication with a narcissist.

*I*n Chapter 6, we delve into the intricate world of communicating with a narcissist and focus on the vital aspect of setting realistic expectations.

When engaging in communication with a narcissist, it's crucial to understand their unique traits and tendencies to effectively manage our own expectations and protect our emotional well-being.

One important aspect of setting realistic expectations is recognizing that narcissists are fundamentally self-centered individuals who prioritize their own needs and desires above others.

They often lack empathy and the ability to genuinely understand or validate the feelings of those around them.

Therefore, expecting them to show empathy, take responsibility for their actions, or consider our perspective is likely to lead to disappointment and frustration.

It's also important to acknowledge that communication with a narcissist is often one-sided and geared towards serving their own agenda.

They may employ manipulation tactics, such as gaslighting or blame-shifting, to deflect responsibility and maintain control.

Understanding these patterns can help us navigate conversations more effectively and resist the temptation to engage in fruitless arguments or attempts to change their behavior.

Setting realistic expectations also involves recognizing that our efforts to communicate and reason with a narcissist may not yield the desired outcomes.

Narcissists have a tendency to resist change or acknowledge their faults, as it threatens their fragile self-image.

Therefore, instead of striving for change or validation from them, we can shift our focus towards our own well-being, personal growth, and establishing healthy boundaries.

By managing our expectations and understanding the limitations of communication with a narcissist, we can free ourselves from the disappointment and emotional turmoil that often accompany these interactions.

This allows us to redirect our energy towards self-care, healing, and building a support network of understanding individuals who can provide the empathy and validation we need.

In Chapter 6, we explore the importance of setting realistic expectations when engaging in communication with a narcissist.

By understanding their self-centered nature, recognizing manipulation tactics, and shifting our focus towards personal growth, we can navigate these interactions more effectively and protect our emotional well-being.

Join us as we continue our journey of unmasking narcissism and discovering empowering strategies to navigate and heal from narcissistic abuse.

Coping with Gaslighting: Providing tools to recognize and counter gaslighting techniques employed by narcissists.

*I*n *Chapter 6, we delve into the challenging realm of communicating with a narcissist and focus on one of their most insidious tactics: gaslighting.*

Gaslighting: is a manipulative technique employed by narcissists to distort and undermine their victim's perception of reality, leaving them confused, doubting themselves, and questioning their sanity.

In this, we provide valuable tools to recognize and counter gaslighting, empowering individuals to regain control over their own truth.

Gaslighting can take various forms, including denying the occurrence of certain events, manipulating facts, or even outrightly contradicting the victim's experiences.

It aims to erode the victim's confidence, diminish their self-worth, and make them dependent on the narcissist for validation and guidance.

Recognizing gaslighting is the first step towards breaking free from its detrimental effects.

One crucial tool to combat gaslighting is maintaining a strong sense of self and trusting your own perceptions.

Narcissists often attempt to distort reality to suit their narrative and gain control.

By staying grounded in your own truth, valuing your emotions and experiences, and seeking validation from trusted sources, you can resist the gaslighting attempts and maintain your mental clarity.

Another effective strategy is documenting incidents and keeping a record of conversations.

Gaslighting thrives on the victim's uncertainty and lack of evidence.

By maintaining a written record of interactions, including dates, times, and details, you can validate your experiences and counter the narcissist's attempts to rewrite history.

Seeking support from a trusted therapist or support group can also be instrumental in coping with gaslighting.

These professionals can provide an objective perspective, validate your experiences, and help you develop coping mechanisms to navigate the challenges posed by a gaslighting narcissist.

Furthermore, it is essential to establish and enforce clear boundaries when communicating with a narcissist.

Setting boundaries helps protect your mental and emotional well-being and prevents the narcissist from manipulating and gaslighting you.

By clearly defining your limits and communicating them assertively, you take back control of the conversation and assert your self-respect.

In Chapter 6, we equip readers with comprehensive tools and strategies to cope with gaslighting techniques employed by narcissists.

By recognizing gaslighting, trusting your own perceptions, documenting incidents, seeking support, and establishing boundaries, you can effectively counter this manipulative tactic and regain your sense of self.

Join us as we continue our journey of unmasking narcissism and discovering empowering strategies to navigate and heal from narcissistic abuse.

Chapter 7: Self-Care and Emotional Healing

Importance of Self-Care: Stressing the significance of self-care in the recovery process.

*I*n Chapter 7, we delve into the vital topic of self-care and its profound impact on the journey of healing and recovery from narcissistic abuse.

Self-care: is not just a trendy buzzword; it is a fundamental pillar that nurtures our well-being and restores our sense of self.

This chapter emphasizes the significance of self-care in the recovery process and provides invaluable insights into how it can be a transformative tool for emotional healing.

When recovering from narcissistic abuse, it is crucial to prioritize self-care as an act of self-love and self-compassion.

The aftermath of abuse can leave deep emotional wounds, ranging from anxiety and depression to feelings of low self-worth.

Self-care acts as a healing balm for these wounds, allowing us to reclaim our personal power and rebuild our lives.

Self-care involves nurturing ourselves physically, emotionally, mentally, and spiritually.

It is about recognizing and honoring our needs, boundaries, and desires.

By engaging in self-care activities, we send a powerful message to ourselves that we deserve love, care, and respect.

It is an act of reclaiming our worth and refusing to let the abuse define us.

Moreover, self-care serves as a protective shield against potential triggers and stressors that may arise during the healing journey.

It provides us with the strength and resilience to navigate challenging emotions and situations.

By taking care of ourselves, we create a safe and nurturing environment where healing can occur.

Self-care practices can take various forms, tailored to individual preferences and needs.

It may include activities such as engaging in hobbies, practicing mindfulness and meditation, maintaining a healthy lifestyle through exercise and proper nutrition, connecting with supportive friends and family, seeking therapy or counseling, and engaging in creative outlets for self-expression.

The key is to identify what brings you joy, peace, and a sense of fulfillment and prioritize those activities in your daily life.

In this chapter, we delve into specific self-care strategies and explore their profound impact on emotional healing.

We provide insights into lesser-known practices that can enhance your self-care routine, nurturing your mind, body, and spirit.

By incorporating these strategies into your life, you will gradually reclaim your sense of self, rebuild your self-esteem, and cultivate a deep sense of well-being.

Join us in Chapter 7 as we highlight the importance of self-care in the recovery process.

Discover empowering strategies to nurture yourself, prioritize your well-being, and embark on a transformative journey of emotional healing.

Let self-care become your guiding compass as you navigate the path to reclaiming your life and embracing a future filled with love, joy, and inner peace.

Self-Care Techniques: Offering a range of self-care strategies such as mindfulness, meditation, exercise, and creative outlets.

Welcome to Chapter 7, where we dive deep into the transformative power of self-care and its role in the journey of healing and recovery from narcissistic abuse.

In this chapter, we explore a wide range of self-care techniques that can empower you to reclaim your well-being and foster emotional healing.

From mindfulness and meditation to exercise and creative outlets, these strategies are carefully curated to provide you with a comprehensive toolkit for self-care.

Mindfulness and meditation are powerful practices that can help you cultivate a sense of inner peace and reconnect with the present moment.

By practicing mindfulness, you can develop awareness of your thoughts, emotions, and bodily sensations, allowing you to better understand and navigate your inner landscape.

Meditation, on the other hand, offers a space for relaxation and self-reflection, enabling you to release stress and cultivate a deeper connection with yourself.

Engaging in regular physical exercise is another essential aspect of self-care.

Exercise not only benefits your physical health but also has a profound impact on your mental and emotional well-being.

It releases endorphins, the body's natural mood boosters, which can help alleviate symptoms of anxiety and depression.

Whether it's going for a brisk walk, practicing yoga, or hitting the gym, finding an exercise routine that suits your preferences and needs can be a game-changer in your healing journey.

Creativity is a powerful outlet for self-expression and emotional release.

Engaging in creative activities, such as painting, writing, dancing, or playing a musical instrument, allows you to tap into your inner world and express your thoughts and emotions in a non-judgmental and cathartic manner.

It can serve as a channel for processing and transforming your experiences, providing a sense of empowerment and healing.

Additionally, incorporating self-care activities into your daily routine can help restore a sense of balance and self-nurturing.

This can include setting aside time for relaxation, indulging in a warm bath or a favorite hobby, spending quality time with loved ones, practicing self-compassion through positive self-talk and affirmations, or engaging in activities that bring you joy and fulfillment.

It's important to note that self-care is a deeply personal journey, and what works for one person may not work for another.

It's about finding the self-care strategies that resonate with you and integrating them into your life in a way that feels authentic and nourishing.

The key is to approach self-care with curiosity and openness, allowing yourself the space to explore and discover what truly supports your healing process.

In Chapter 7, we provide in-depth guidance on each self-care technique, exploring their benefits, and offering practical tips on how to incorporate them into your daily life.

We also share lesser-known techniques and insights that can enhance your self-care practice and foster emotional healing.

By immersing yourself in the world of self-care, you will unlock a powerful tool for self-empowerment, resilience, and inner transformation.

Join us in Chapter 7 as we delve into the realm of self-care techniques.

Discover the practices that resonate with you, cultivate a nurturing relationship with yourself, and embark on a journey of emotional healing and self-discovery.

Let self-care become your compass as you navigate the path toward reclaiming your well-being and embracing a life of empowerment and wholeness.

Managing Stress and Anxiety: Providing practical tips for managing stress and anxiety symptoms resulting from narcissistic abuse.

Welcome to Chapter 7, where we delve into the vital importance of self-care and its role in the journey of healing and recovery from narcissistic abuse.

In this chapter, we focus on a crucial aspect of self-care: managing stress and anxiety, which are common symptoms resulting from the traumatic experiences of narcissistic abuse.

We provide practical tips and techniques that can empower you to effectively navigate and alleviate these challenging emotions, allowing you to regain a sense of inner calm and emotional well-being.

Managing stress and anxiety: begins with self-awareness.

It's essential to recognize the triggers that contribute to your stress and anxiety levels.

These triggers can vary from person to person, as everyone's experiences and sensitivities are unique.

By identifying and understanding your personal triggers, you can develop targeted strategies to address them and minimize their impact on your well-being.

One effective technique for managing stress and anxiety is the practice of deep breathing and relaxation exercises.

Deep breathing techniques:, such as diaphragmatic breathing, can help regulate your nervous system and induce a state of relaxation.

By focusing on your breath and consciously slowing it down, you can activate the body's natural relaxation response and reduce the physiological symptoms of stress and anxiety.

Another valuable strategy is the cultivation of a support network.

Connecting with empathetic and understanding individuals who have also experienced narcissistic abuse can provide a safe and validating space for sharing your thoughts and emotions.

Support groups:, therapy, or online communities can be invaluable resources for finding solace, guidance, and encouragement during your healing journey.

Engaging in activities that promote self-soothing and relaxation is an integral part of managing stress and anxiety.

These activities can vary depending on your personal preferences and interests.

Some individuals find solace in practicing mindfulness and meditation, while others find comfort in engaging in physical activities like yoga or taking soothing baths.

Exploring different self-soothing techniques can help you discover what works best for you and aids in creating a calming environment for emotional healing.

It's important to acknowledge that managing stress and anxiety is an ongoing process that requires patience and self-compassion.

It may take time to find the strategies that resonate with you and provide the most significant relief.

Additionally, seeking professional support from therapists or counselors who specialize in trauma and abuse can offer tailored guidance and therapeutic interventions to assist you in managing and overcoming stress and anxiety.

In Chapter 7, we provide comprehensive guidance on managing stress and anxiety, sharing lesser-known tips and techniques that can complement traditional approaches.

We explore the mind-body connection and how nurturing your physical well-being can positively impact your emotional resilience.

Through our detailed insights and practical advice, you'll gain a deeper understanding of the strategies that can support you in managing stress and anxiety, enabling you to reclaim your inner peace and emotional stability.

Join us in Chapter 7 as we embark on the journey of self-care and emotional healing.

Discover the transformative power of managing stress and anxiety, and equip yourself with the tools and knowledge to cultivate emotional well-being.

By incorporating these strategies into your daily life, you will be taking proactive steps towards healing, empowerment, and creating a brighter future beyond the shadows of narcissistic abuse.

Seeking Professional Help: Encouraging readers to seek therapy, counseling, or support groups for additional guidance and healing.

Welcome to Chapter 7, where we explore the critical role of self-care and emotional healing in navigating the complex aftermath of narcissistic abuse.

In this chapter, we shine a light on the significance of seeking professional help as an empowering step towards healing and recovery.

While self-care practices and strategies are invaluable, the guidance and support of trained professionals can provide an additional layer of understanding, validation, and specialized expertise.

Therapy and counseling offer a safe and confidential space where you can openly explore your experiences, emotions, and challenges related to narcissistic abuse.

A qualified therapist or counselor with expertise in trauma and abuse can help you navigate the complexities of your healing journey, offering tailored guidance and evidence-based interventions.

They can assist in unraveling the intricate emotional dynamics resulting from the abuse, helping you regain a sense of self-worth, rebuild trust in yourself and others, and develop healthier coping mechanisms.

Support groups, both in-person and online, provide a unique opportunity to connect with individuals who have undergone similar experiences.

These groups offer a sense of community, understanding, and validation, as well as a platform for sharing stories, insights, and coping strategies.

Engaging with others who have faced narcissistic abuse can be immensely healing, as it counters the isolation and self-doubt often perpetuated by narcissistic manipulations.

It is important to note that seeking professional help is not a sign of weakness but rather a courageous act of self-care and self-empowerment.

These professionals are equipped with the knowledge and tools to guide you through the healing process, address any lingering trauma or emotional wounds, and help you rebuild a resilient and fulfilling life.

When seeking professional help, it is crucial to find a therapist, counselor, or support group that specializes in trauma, abuse, and narcissistic dynamics.

They should have experience in working with survivors of narcissistic abuse and a compassionate approach that prioritizes your well-being.

Take the time to research and interview potential professionals to ensure they are the right fit for your needs.

In Chapter 7, we delve deeper into the importance of seeking professional help and provide guidance on finding the right support for your healing journey.

We explore the lesser-known benefits of therapy, counseling, and support groups, shedding light on the transformative potential of these resources.

By combining self-care practices with professional guidance, you can cultivate a comprehensive approach to healing and regain control over your emotional well-being.

Join us in Chapter 7 as we embrace the path of self-care and emotional healing.

Discover the profound impact that seeking professional help can have on your recovery and growth.

By incorporating these empowering strategies into your journey, you can find solace, understanding, and renewed strength as you navigate the complexities of healing from narcissistic abuse.

Remember, healing is a deeply personal and transformative process, and professional support can serve as a guiding light on your path to reclaiming your life.

Chapter 8: Breaking Free: Detaching from the Narcissist

Emotionally Detaching: Step-by-step guidance on detaching emotionally from the narcissist and their manipulative tactics.

Welcome to Chapter 8, where we embark on a journey of breaking free from the grip of the narcissist and reclaiming our emotional well-being.

In this chapter, we delve into the process of emotionally detaching from the narcissist and provide you with step-by-step guidance to navigate their manipulative tactics.

Emotional detachment is a crucial step in the healing process, allowing you to regain control over your emotions, thoughts, and actions.

It involves creating a healthy distance from the narcissist's toxic influence, breaking free from their manipulative web, and reclaiming your autonomy and self-worth.

While detaching emotionally may seem daunting, it is an empowering strategy that empowers you to set boundaries, prioritize your needs, and establish a new sense of self.

To begin the process of emotional detachment, it is essential to recognize and understand the manipulative tactics employed by narcissists.

These tactics can range from gaslighting and manipulation to guilt-tripping and triangulation.

By gaining awareness of these tactics, you can begin to identify when they are being used against you and disengage from their harmful effects.

Setting clear boundaries is another vital aspect of emotional detachment.

Establishing and enforcing boundaries sends a powerful message to the narcissist that their manipulative behaviors will no longer be tolerated.

It is important to communicate your boundaries assertively and consistently, and to be prepared for pushback or attempts to violate them.

Remember, setting boundaries is an act of self-care and self-respect, and it is crucial in breaking free from the narcissist's control.

Building a strong support network is also instrumental in the process of emotional detachment.

Surrounding yourself with understanding and empathetic individuals who validate your experiences can provide invaluable support.

Seek out trusted friends, family members, or support groups who can offer a safe space to express your emotions and provide guidance and encouragement throughout your journey.

Practicing self-care is essential during the process of emotional detachment.

Engage in activities that bring you joy, promote self-reflection, and nurture your well-being.

This may include engaging in hobbies, practicing mindfulness and meditation, seeking professional help, or engaging in physical exercise.

Self-care allows you to reconnect with yourself, rebuild your self-esteem, and cultivate resilience in the face of the narcissist's attempts to regain control.

In Chapter 8, we guide you through the intricate process of emotionally detaching from the narcissist.

Our step-by-step approach offers practical strategies and insights to help you navigate the challenges and setbacks that may arise along the way.

By breaking free from the narcissist's grip, you can reclaim your power, restore your emotional well-being, and forge a path towards a fulfilling and authentic life.

Join us in Chapter 8 as we embark on the journey of detaching emotionally from the narcissist.

Discover the empowering strategies and tools that will guide you towards a life free from manipulation and control.

By embracing the process of emotional detachment, you can break free from the toxic cycle and pave the way for a brighter future filled with self-empowerment and personal growth.

Remember, you deserve to live a life free from the narcissist's influence, and this chapter will serve as your compass on the path to freedom.

Physical Separation: Strategies for creating physical distance and minimizing contact with the narcissist.

Welcome to Chapter 8, where we delve into the powerful process of breaking free from the narcissist's grip and reclaiming our lives.

In this chapter, we focus on the essential strategy of physical separation, providing you with comprehensive guidance and empowering techniques to create physical distance and minimize contact with the narcissist.

Physical separation plays a crucial role in the healing journey, as it allows for a much-needed space to rebuild your sense of self and regain control over your life.

While it may not always be possible to completely cut off all contact, implementing strategies to minimize interaction and establish boundaries can be immensely liberating.

One effective strategy for physical separation is to limit or block communication channels with the narcissist.

This may involve changing your phone number, blocking their email address, or utilizing privacy settings on social media platforms.

By reducing avenues of communication, you can create a protective barrier that minimizes their ability to intrude into your life and manipulate your emotions.

Additionally, restructuring your physical environment can aid in creating distance.

This may include moving to a new home or rearranging living spaces to eliminate reminders of the narcissist.

Surrounding yourself with a supportive and nurturing environment can facilitate healing and provide a sanctuary for your emotional well-being.

Seeking support from a professional, such as a therapist or counselor, can be immensely beneficial during this process.

They can offer guidance tailored to your specific situation, providing tools and techniques to navigate the challenges of physical separation.

They can also help you develop coping mechanisms to manage any feelings of guilt, fear, or uncertainty that may arise during this transformative period.

While physical separation is a critical step, it is important to acknowledge that it can be emotionally challenging.

You may experience feelings of grief, loss, and even moments of doubt.

It is crucial to be patient with yourself and seek support from your support network.

Engaging in self-care activities, such as exercise, journaling, or engaging in hobbies, can provide a much-needed outlet for processing emotions and fostering healing.

Remember, physical separation is a powerful act of self-preservation and a necessary step towards reclaiming your life and well-being.

It is an opportunity to establish new boundaries, rebuild your sense of self, and create a space where your authentic self can flourish.

By implementing the strategies outlined in this chapter, you can take decisive steps towards breaking free from the narcissist's influence and embarking on a journey of personal growth and empowerment.

Join us in Chapter 8 as we explore the transformative process of physical separation from the narcissist.

Discover the empowering strategies and techniques that will help you create distance and minimize contact.

By embracing physical separation, you can pave the way for a life free from the toxic cycle of narcissistic abuse and embark on a path towards healing and self-discovery.

Remember, you deserve a life filled with peace, happiness, and authenticity, and this chapter will serve as your guide towards achieving that liberation.

Establishing No-Contact: Exploring the benefits of implementing and maintaining a no-contact rule for personal well-being.

Welcome to Chapter 8, where we embark on a powerful journey of breaking free from the narcissist's grip and reclaiming our lives.

In this chapter, we delve into the empowering strategy of establishing a no-contact rule, exploring its benefits for personal well-being and offering invaluable insights to navigate this transformative process.

Implementing and maintaining a no-contact rule can be a vital step in the healing process after experiencing narcissistic abuse.

It involves cutting off all forms of communication and contact with the narcissist, creating a definitive boundary that prioritizes your emotional well-being and protects you from further harm.

While it may be challenging, the benefits of establishing a no-contact rule are immense.

One of the key advantages of no-contact is the restoration of your sense of self.

Narcissistic abuse often erodes our self-esteem and distorts our perception of reality.

By severing ties with the narcissist, you create an opportunity to rediscover your authentic self and rebuild your identity without their influence.

Maintaining no-contact also prevents the narcissist from continuing their cycle of manipulation and control.

Narcissists thrive on power and dominance, and by breaking free from their grasp, you take away their ability to exert control over your emotions and actions.

It allows you to reclaim your autonomy and assert your boundaries, fostering a sense of empowerment and self-respect.

Furthermore, implementing a no-contact rule provides a space for healing and recovery.

It allows you to focus on your own emotional well-being without being entangled in the toxic dynamics of the relationship.

This separation provides an opportunity to process the trauma, heal from the emotional wounds, and gradually restore your mental and emotional balance.

It is important to note that maintaining no-contact may require additional steps, such as blocking the narcissist's phone number, email address, and social media accounts.

It also involves establishing boundaries with mutual acquaintances or family members who may still be in contact with the narcissist.

Surrounding yourself with a supportive network and seeking professional guidance can provide the necessary tools and emotional support during this challenging but transformative phase.

While establishing and maintaining a no-contact rule can be difficult, it is crucial to prioritize your own well-being.

Setbacks and challenges may arise along the way, but remember that you are taking a courageous step towards reclaiming your life and embracing your true self.

Engaging in self-care practices, therapy, and support groups can aid in the healing process and provide the necessary tools to navigate the emotional complexities of detaching from the narcissist.

Join us in Chapter 8 as we explore the transformative journey of establishing a no-contact rule.

Discover the empowering benefits of cutting off contact with the narcissist and learn effective strategies to maintain this boundary.

By embracing no-contact, you can create a space for healing, personal growth, and a life free from the toxic grip of narcissistic abuse.

Remember, you deserve to thrive, and this chapter will serve as your guide towards breaking free and reclaiming your happiness and well-being.

Dealing with Hoovering: Providing insights into how to handle hoovering attempts, which are the narcissist's efforts to draw the victim back into the abusive relationship.

Welcome to Chapter 8, where we embark on a transformative journey of breaking free from the narcissist's grip and reclaiming our lives.

In this chapter, we will explore a crucial aspect of detaching from the narcissist: dealing with hoovering.

Hoovering: refers to the manipulative attempts made by the narcissist to draw the victim back into the abusive relationship.

By understanding hoovering tactics and implementing effective strategies, we can protect ourselves and maintain our progress on the path to healing and empowerment.

Hoovering can take various forms, such as sudden acts of kindness, promises of change, or even threats and intimidation.

These tactics are designed to exploit our vulnerabilities and trigger emotional reactions that might entice us to re-engage with the narcissist.

It is essential to recognize that hoovering is not a genuine attempt at reconciliation or change but rather a ploy to regain control and continue the cycle of abuse.

One key strategy for dealing with hoovering is to stay grounded in our knowledge and awareness of narcissistic behavior.

Educating ourselves about narcissism and understanding the manipulative tactics employed by narcissists can provide us with a solid foundation to recognize and resist hoovering attempts.

This knowledge empowers us to see through the façade and stay committed to our healing journey.

Setting clear boundaries is another crucial aspect of handling hoovering attempts.

By establishing firm boundaries, we send a strong message that we will not tolerate further manipulation or abuse.

This includes maintaining no-contact and refusing to engage in any form of communication with the narcissist.

It may be necessary to block their phone number, email address, and social media profiles to ensure they cannot reach us.

In addition to setting boundaries, it is essential to surround ourselves with a supportive network of friends, family, or a therapist who can provide guidance and validation during this challenging time.

Sharing our experiences and feelings with trusted individuals can provide emotional strength and reinforce our commitment to breaking free from the narcissist's influence.

Self-care practices play a vital role in dealing with hoovering attempts as well.

Engaging in activities that nurture our physical, mental, and emotional well-being can help us stay resilient and focused on our healing journey.

This may include practicing mindfulness, engaging in regular exercise, journaling, or pursuing creative outlets that allow us to express ourselves and process our emotions.

Remember that dealing with hoovering attempts may evoke a range of emotions, including confusion, guilt, or longing.

It is crucial to validate these feelings and remind ourselves of the reasons we chose to break free.

Healing from narcissistic abuse is a process that requires patience, self-compassion, and a commitment to our own well-being.

In this chapter, we will delve deeper into the nuances of hoovering, providing valuable insights and practical strategies to handle these manipulative attempts effectively.

By arming ourselves with knowledge, setting boundaries, seeking support, and prioritizing self-care, we can navigate the complexities of hoovering and continue on our path to healing and empowerment.

Join us in Chapter 8 as we explore the empowering journey of breaking free from the narcissist's grip and maintaining our progress.

Discover the strategies and tools to handle hoovering attempts with confidence and resilience.

Together, we can overcome the challenges and reclaim our lives, emerging stronger, wiser, and free from the clutches of narcissistic abuse.

Chapter 9: The Healing Journey

Recognizing and Processing Emotions: Assisting readers in identifying and acknowledging their emotions related to the abuse, such as anger, grief, and betrayal.

Welcome to Chapter 9, where we embark on a profound exploration of the healing journey after narcissistic abuse.

In this chapter, we will delve into a crucial aspect of healing: recognizing and processing emotions.

The aftermath of narcissistic abuse can leave us with a complex mix of emotions, including anger, grief, betrayal, and a myriad of other feelings that may be challenging to navigate.

By developing a deeper understanding of these emotions and implementing effective strategies, we can pave the way for true healing and emotional well-being.

One of the first steps in the healing journey is to recognize and acknowledge the emotions that arise as a result of the abuse.

It is common for survivors to experience intense anger towards the narcissist, as they come to terms with the manipulation, deceit, and harm inflicted upon them.

This anger is a natural response to the violation of trust and the realization of the narcissist's true intentions.

It is important to give ourselves permission to feel and express this anger in healthy and constructive ways, such as through journaling, physical exercise, or seeking the support of a therapist.

Grief is another emotion that often accompanies the healing process.

Survivors may grieve the loss of the idealized image they once had of the narcissist, the shattered dreams, and the time and energy invested in the relationship.

It is important to honor this grief and allow ourselves to mourn the loss.

This may involve creating rituals of closure, writing letters to the narcissist (without sending them), or engaging in activities that promote self-expression and emotional release.

Betrayal is another complex emotion that can arise during the healing journey.

Survivors often grapple with feelings of betrayal, as they come to terms with the narcissist's manipulation, deceit, and disregard for their well-being.

It is crucial to validate these feelings and understand that the betrayal is a reflection of the narcissist's character and not a reflection of our worth.

Engaging in self-compassion practices, such as self-forgiveness and self-care, can help in processing and healing from the deep wounds of betrayal.

Processing these emotions is not an easy task, and it requires patience, self-compassion, and a supportive network.

Seeking the guidance of a therapist or counselor who specializes in narcissistic abuse can provide invaluable support in navigating these complex emotions.

These professionals can offer a safe space to express ourselves, validate our experiences, and provide strategies for emotional healing.

Additionally, engaging in self-care practices is vital during the healing journey.

Taking care of our physical, mental, and emotional well-being can support the processing of emotions and promote overall healing.

This may include activities such as meditation, mindfulness exercises, engaging in hobbies or creative outlets, practicing self-care rituals, or spending time in nature.

These practices not only provide solace and restoration but also help in developing a deeper connection with ourselves and our inner strength.

In Chapter 9, we will delve deeper into the intricacies of recognizing and processing emotions related to narcissistic abuse.

By developing a comprehensive understanding of our emotional landscape and implementing effective strategies, we can pave the way for profound healing and emotional liberation.

Join us as we navigate the complex terrain of emotions, empowering ourselves to reclaim our lives and forge a path towards a brighter future.

Remember, the healing journey is unique for each individual, and it is important to honor our own pace and process.

By acknowledging and processing our emotions, we can release the weight of the abuse and create space for genuine healing and growth.

Together, let us embrace our emotions, find solace in our resilience, and emerge stronger than ever before on this transformative healing journey.

Tools for Self-Reflection and Self-Awareness: Introducing practices like journaling, therapy, and introspection to promote self-awareness and personal growth.

Welcome to Chapter 9, where we embark on a transformative exploration of the healing journey after narcissistic abuse.

In this chapter, we will delve into the powerful tools of self-reflection and self-awareness, which play a crucial role in our personal growth and healing.

By incorporating practices such as journaling, therapy, and introspection into our lives, we can foster a deeper understanding of ourselves, unravel the effects of narcissistic abuse, and cultivate lasting healing and empowerment.

One of the most effective tools for self-reflection and self-awareness is journaling.

Through the act of writing, we create a safe space to express our thoughts, emotions, and experiences.

Journaling allows us to process and make sense of the complex emotions that arise from the trauma of narcissistic abuse.

It provides an outlet for our innermost thoughts and feelings, helping us gain clarity, release pent-up emotions, and gain a deeper understanding of ourselves.

By regularly journaling, we can track our progress, identify patterns, and gain insights into our healing journey.

Therapy is another invaluable tool for self-reflection and self-awareness.

Working with a qualified therapist who specializes in narcissistic abuse can provide a supportive and non-judgmental environment to explore our experiences, emotions, and belief systems.

A therapist can help us uncover deep-rooted wounds, challenge distorted beliefs instilled by the narcissist, and guide us towards healing and personal growth.

Through therapeutic modalities such as cognitive-behavioral therapy (CBT), dialectical behavior therapy (DBT), or trauma-focused therapy, we can develop coping mechanisms, build resilience, and redefine our self-worth.

Introspection, or deep self-reflection, is a practice that encourages us to examine our thoughts, emotions, and behaviors in a mindful and non-judgmental way.

It involves setting aside dedicated time for self-exploration, asking ourselves meaningful questions, and listening to our inner wisdom.

Introspection allows us to uncover subconscious beliefs, motivations, and patterns that may have contributed to our vulnerability to narcissistic abuse.

By cultivating self-awareness through introspection, we can identify areas for personal growth, develop healthier boundaries, and build a stronger sense of self.

Incorporating these tools for self-reflection and self-awareness into our healing journey is a transformative and empowering process.

It allows us to reclaim our identities, heal from the wounds of narcissistic abuse, and cultivate a deep connection with ourselves.

By gaining a deeper understanding of our triggers, vulnerabilities, and strengths, we can make informed choices, establish healthier relationships, and navigate life with resilience and authenticity.

Remember, the healing journey is unique for each individual, and it is important to honor our own process.

By embracing practices such as journaling, therapy, and introspection, we empower ourselves to embark on a path of self-discovery and growth.

These tools provide us with the guidance and insights necessary to break free from the chains of narcissistic abuse and create a life of authenticity, joy, and inner peace.

In Chapter 9, we will explore these tools for self-reflection and self-awareness in greater detail.

Together, let us embark on this profound journey of self-discovery, healing, and personal transformation.

By harnessing the power of self-reflection and self-awareness, we can navigate the healing journey with courage, compassion, and a renewed sense of purpose.

Join us as we unlock the door to our true selves and embrace the limitless possibilities that lie ahead.

Healing Trauma: Exploring various trauma healing modalities, such as EMDR (Eye Movement Desensitization and Reprocessing) and somatic experiencing, to address the impact of narcissistic abuse.

Welcome to Chapter 9, where we embark on a profound exploration of healing trauma after narcissistic abuse.

In this chapter, we will delve into the transformative modalities that can help us address the deep-seated impact of narcissistic abuse and reclaim our lives.

By exploring trauma healing techniques such as EMDR (Eye Movement Desensitization and Reprocessing) and somatic experiencing, we can effectively release the emotional and physiological wounds inflicted by narcissistic abuse and pave the way for lasting recovery and empowerment.

EMDR:, which stands for Eye Movement Desensitization and Reprocessing, is a well-established therapeutic approach designed to address the effects of trauma.

It utilizes bilateral stimulation, such as eye movements, to facilitate the reprocessing of distressing memories and associated beliefs.

EMDR helps to desensitize the emotional charge attached to traumatic experiences, allowing individuals to reprocess and integrate these experiences in a healthier way.

By engaging in EMDR therapy with a trained professional, we can effectively release the trauma stored within our minds and bodies, leading to significant healing and resolution.

Somatic: experiencing is another powerful modality that focuses on the body's role in trauma healing.

Developed by Peter A. Levine, somatic experiencing recognizes that trauma is not just a psychological experience but also an embodied one.

It emphasizes the importance of releasing and regulating the physiological responses associated with trauma.

Through somatic experiencing, we learn to reconnect with our bodies, release trapped energy, and restore a sense of safety and empowerment.

By working with a somatic experiencing practitioner, we can address the physical and energetic imprints of narcissistic abuse and promote deep healing and restoration.

It is important to note that the healing journey after narcissistic abuse is unique for each individual, and what works for one person may not work for another.

Therefore, it is crucial to seek guidance from qualified professionals who specialize in trauma healing.

These professionals can provide personalized strategies tailored to our specific needs and empower us to navigate the complex terrain of trauma with compassion and expertise.

In addition to EMDR and somatic experiencing, there are a variety of other trauma healing modalities available, such as cognitive-behavioral therapy (CBT), art therapy, mindfulness practices, and support groups.

The key is to find the approach or combination of approaches that resonate with us personally and support our individual healing journey.

By exploring these modalities under the guidance of trained professionals, we can gradually release the grip of trauma, reclaim our power, and embark on a path of profound healing and transformation.

Chapter 9 will delve deeper into these trauma healing modalities, providing insights, techniques, and resources to support our healing journey.

Together, let us embrace the power of EMDR, somatic experiencing, and other trauma healing approaches as we navigate the complexities of narcissistic abuse recovery.

By honoring our unique experiences and seeking the appropriate support, we can pave the way for profound healing, resilience, and a future filled with authentic self-expression and joy.

Reconnecting with Authentic Self: Guiding readers in rediscovering their true identity and reclaiming their sense of self-worth.

Welcome to Chapter 9, where we embark on a transformative exploration of reconnecting with our authentic selves after the devastating effects of narcissistic abuse.

In this chapter, we will delve into empowering strategies and insights that will guide you on a journey of rediscovering your true identity, reclaiming your sense of self-worth, and building a foundation of resilience and empowerment.

Narcissistic abuse can leave us feeling lost, disconnected, and uncertain of our own worth.

It can erode our self-esteem, distort our perception of ourselves, and leave us questioning our own identity.

However, the healing journey offers an opportunity to re-establish a deep and meaningful connection with our authentic selves, unburdened by the manipulative influence of the narcissist.

Rediscovering your authentic self begins with self-reflection and self-exploration.

It's about taking the time to examine your values, passions, and interests outside of the narcissistic dynamic.

This process may involve exploring new hobbies, engaging in creative outlets, or revisiting activities that once brought you joy.

By reconnecting with your own unique desires and preferences, you can rebuild a sense of self that is independent of the narcissist's influence.

Another essential aspect of reconnecting with your authentic self is setting boundaries and asserting your needs and desires.

It's crucial to honor your own values and priorities, even if they differ from what the narcissist expects or demands.

By establishing healthy boundaries, you create a space where your true self can flourish, free from the constant scrutiny and manipulation of the narcissist.

Self-care practices play a vital role in this healing journey.

Engaging in activities that nourish your mind, body, and spirit is essential for reconnecting with your authentic self.

This may include practicing mindfulness, engaging in regular exercise, seeking therapy or counseling, or connecting with supportive communities and networks.

By prioritizing self-care, you signal to yourself that your needs are valid and deserve attention and nurturing.

It's important to remember that reconnecting with your authentic self is a process that requires patience, self-compassion, and support.

Surrounding yourself with a network of understanding and empathetic individuals can provide a safe space for exploration and healing.

Support groups, therapy, or counseling can offer guidance and validation as you navigate this deeply personal journey.

In Chapter 9, we will dive deeper into strategies, techniques, and resources that will empower you on your healing journey of reconnecting with your authentic self.

Through self-reflection, boundary-setting, self-care, and support, you can rediscover your inherent worth, embrace your unique identity, and build a life filled with authenticity and fulfillment.

Remember, the healing journey is yours to navigate, and there is no one-size-fits-all approach.

Embrace the uniqueness of your experience and allow yourself the freedom to discover and celebrate your authentic self.

Let us embark on this transformative chapter together, as we reclaim our sense of self-worth, embrace our true identities, and forge a future of healing, empowerment, and joy.

Chapter 10: Rebuilding Self-Esteem and Confidence

Challenging Negative Self-Beliefs: Helping readers identify and challenge the negative beliefs instilled by the narcissist, replacing them with empowering and positive self-perceptions.

Welcome to Chapter 10, where we embark on the empowering journey of rebuilding self-esteem and confidence after the trauma of narcissistic abuse.

In this chapter, we will explore strategies and insights to help you challenge and overcome the negative self-beliefs that have been instilled by the narcissist, replacing them with empowering and positive self-perceptions.

Narcissistic abuse can leave deep scars on our self-esteem and confidence.

The constant criticism, gaslighting, and manipulation can erode our sense of self-worth, leaving us feeling inadequate, unworthy, and full of self-doubt.

However, the healing process involves recognizing that these negative beliefs are a product of the narcissist's tactics and not a reflection of our true value.

The first step in challenging negative self-beliefs is self-awareness.

It's essential to identify and become aware of the negative thoughts and beliefs that arise within you.

These beliefs may manifest as self-critical thoughts, feelings of shame or guilt, or a persistent inner voice telling you that you are not enough.

By shining a light on these beliefs, you can start to examine them objectively and question their validity.

Next, it's crucial to challenge these negative beliefs by replacing them with empowering and positive self-perceptions.

This process requires self-compassion, patience, and a commitment to reframing your mindset.

One effective technique is to gather evidence that contradicts the negative beliefs.

For example, if you believe you are incompetent, make a list of your achievements and strengths to remind yourself of your capabilities.

Cognitive-behavioral therapy (CBT) can be a valuable resource in challenging negative self-beliefs.

Working with a therapist trained in CBT techniques can help you identify cognitive distortions and develop healthier thought patterns.

Through cognitive restructuring, you can challenge irrational beliefs and replace them with more realistic and empowering perspectives.

Another effective strategy is to surround yourself with positive and supportive influences.

Seek out relationships and communities that uplift and validate you.

Engage in activities that bring you joy and boost your self-esteem.

Surrounding yourself with positivity can counteract the negative beliefs implanted by the narcissist and reinforce a healthier self-perception.

Self-affirmations and positive self-talk can also play a significant role in rebuilding self-esteem and confidence.

Practice speaking kind and affirming words to yourself, acknowledging your strengths and progress.

Remember, self-compassion and self-acceptance are key components of this process.

Rebuilding self-esteem and confidence is a journey that requires time, effort, and self-compassion.

It's important to acknowledge that setbacks may occur, but they do not define your worth or progress.

Embrace the small victories and celebrate your resilience.

With each step forward, you reclaim your power and build a solid foundation of self-esteem and confidence.

In Chapter 10, we will delve deeper into the strategies, techniques, and resources that will empower you to rebuild your self-esteem and confidence.

By challenging negative self-beliefs, nurturing self-compassion, and surrounding yourself with positivity, you can cultivate a strong sense of self-worth and confidently navigate the path to healing and personal growth.

Remember, you are deserving of love, respect, and happiness.

You possess unique qualities and strengths that no one can diminish.

Together, let us embark on this transformative chapter of rebuilding self-esteem and confidence, as we embrace our true worth and create a future filled with self-assurance and empowerment.

Practicing Self-Compassion and Self-Love: Introducing self-compassion exercises and techniques to foster self-acceptance, self-forgiveness, and self-care.

Welcome to Chapter 10, where we embark on a transformative journey of rebuilding self-esteem and confidence after the devastating effects of narcissistic abuse.

In this chapter, we will explore empowering strategies and techniques that focus on practicing self-compassion and self-love.

By fostering self-acceptance, self-forgiveness, and self-care, we can reclaim our sense of worth and rebuild a strong foundation for our emotional well-being.

Narcissistic abuse often leaves us feeling broken, unworthy, and disconnected from our true selves.

The constant criticism, manipulation, and invalidation can chip away at our self-esteem, leaving us in desperate need of healing and nurturing.

Practicing self-compassion is an essential step in this healing process.

Self-compassion involves extending kindness, understanding, and acceptance towards ourselves, especially during times of pain and difficulty.

It is about treating ourselves with the same compassion and care that we would offer to a loved one in need.

By embracing self-compassion, we can create a safe and nurturing space within ourselves, free from self-judgment and self-criticism.

One effective technique to cultivate self-compassion is through self-compassion exercises.

These exercises may include guided meditations, writing self-compassionate letters, or engaging in soothing self-care practices.

By incorporating these exercises into our daily lives, we can shift our mindset and develop a more compassionate and loving relationship with ourselves.

Self-forgiveness is another crucial aspect of rebuilding self-esteem and confidence.

It involves releasing ourselves from the burdens of self-blame and guilt for the abuse endured.

Remember, the responsibility for the abuse lies solely with the narcissist.

By practicing self-forgiveness, we free ourselves from the weight of the past and allow space for healing and growth.

In addition to self-compassion and self-forgiveness, self-care plays a vital role in rebuilding self-esteem and confidence.

Self-care involves nurturing our physical, emotional, and mental well-being.

It encompasses activities that bring us joy, relaxation, and rejuvenation.

Engaging in self-care practices can replenish our energy, boost our mood, and reaffirm our self-worth.

Self-love is the foundation upon which self-esteem and confidence are built.

It involves developing a deep sense of respect, acceptance, and appreciation for ourselves.

Cultivating self-love requires challenging the negative self-talk and embracing our strengths, talents, and unique qualities.

It involves setting boundaries, prioritizing our needs, and surrounding ourselves with positive influences.

Remember, the journey of rebuilding self-esteem and confidence is a personal and unique one.

It may take time, patience, and support from loved ones or professionals.

However, by practicing self-compassion, self-forgiveness, and self-care, we can gradually restore our sense of worth and reclaim our authentic selves.

In Chapter 10, we will explore various self-compassion exercises, techniques, and self-care practices that will empower you to rebuild your self-esteem and confidence.

By nurturing self-acceptance, practicing forgiveness, and embracing self-love, you will discover a newfound strength and resilience within yourself.

Together, let us embark on this transformative chapter of healing, as we honor our worth, embrace self-compassion, and create a future filled with self-love and confidence.

Setting Achievable Goals: Assisting readers in setting realistic goals and developing action plans to rebuild their lives after narcissistic abuse.

Welcome to Chapter 10, where we embark on a transformative journey of rebuilding self-esteem and confidence after the devastating effects of narcissistic abuse.

In this chapter, we will delve into empowering strategies and techniques that focus on setting achievable goals and developing action plans to rebuild our lives.

Narcissistic abuse can leave us feeling lost and overwhelmed, unsure of where to begin in our healing process.

Setting achievable goals is a crucial step in reclaiming our sense of purpose and regaining control over our lives.

These goals serve as beacons of hope, guiding us towards a brighter and more empowered future.

When setting goals after narcissistic abuse, it is important to start small and be realistic.

Begin by identifying specific areas of your life that you would like to improve or rebuild.

It could be anything from building new relationships, pursuing a career change, or rediscovering hobbies and passions that were suppressed during the abusive relationship.

Once you have identified your areas of focus, break them down into smaller, manageable goals.

This approach allows you to make progress step by step, building confidence along the way.

For example, if your goal is to build new relationships, start by attending social events or joining interest-based groups to expand your social network.

This incremental approach increases the likelihood of success and prevents overwhelm.

Action plans are essential tools in achieving your goals.

They provide structure and guidance, ensuring that you stay on track and make consistent progress.

Start by outlining the specific actions you need to take to reach your goals.

Break them down into actionable steps and assign realistic timelines to each step.

This helps to create a sense of accountability and motivation.

It is important to remember that everyone's healing journey is unique.

Be gentle with yourself and allow for flexibility in your goals and action plans.

Healing takes time, and setbacks are a normal part of the process.

Adapt and adjust your goals as needed, making sure they align with your evolving needs and aspirations.

As you work towards your goals, celebrate your achievements along the way, no matter how small they may seem.

Each step forward is a testament to your strength and resilience.

Surround yourself with a support network of trusted friends, family, or professionals who can provide encouragement and guidance throughout your journey.

In Chapter 10, we will explore strategies for setting achievable goals and developing action plans tailored to your individual needs.

By setting realistic goals, breaking them down into manageable steps, and implementing action plans, you will gain a sense of direction and purpose in rebuilding your life after narcissistic abuse.

Remember, the power to rebuild and thrive lies within you.

You have the strength to overcome the effects of narcissistic abuse and create a fulfilling future.

Let us embark on this chapter of empowerment, as we set achievable goals, develop action plans, and navigate our way towards renewed self-esteem and confidence.

Celebrating Progress: Encouraging readers to acknowledge their accomplishments, no matter how small, and celebrate their growth and resilience.

Welcome to Chapter 10, a pivotal chapter in our journey towards healing and reclaiming our sense of self.

In this chapter, we will explore the empowering strategy of celebrating progress, emphasizing the importance of acknowledging our accomplishments, no matter how small, and honoring our growth and resilience.

After enduring narcissistic abuse, it is common to feel a sense of depletion and self-doubt.

Rebuilding self-esteem and confidence requires us to recognize and appreciate our progress along the way.

By celebrating our achievements, we validate our efforts and reaffirm our worthiness.

It is crucial to understand that progress comes in various forms.

Sometimes it may be a significant milestone, while at other times, it could be a small step towards healing.

Regardless of the size or magnitude, each accomplishment contributes to our overall growth and deserves recognition.

As we navigate our healing journey, it is essential to cultivate a mindset of self-compassion and self-acknowledgment.

Often, we tend to downplay our achievements or compare ourselves to others, diminishing the significance of our progress.

However, true healing lies in embracing and honoring our individual journeys.

One effective way to celebrate progress is by keeping a journal or gratitude log.

Take a moment each day to reflect on your accomplishments, no matter how trivial they may seem.

It could be a new boundary set, a healthy coping mechanism practiced, or a moment of self-care indulgence.

By documenting these moments, you create a tangible reminder of your growth and resilience.

Another powerful way to celebrate progress is by sharing your achievements with a supportive community.

Connect with others who have experienced similar challenges and share your journey.

Online support groups or therapy sessions can provide a safe space for you to express your accomplishments and receive validation from others who understand the depth of your experience.

In addition, treating yourself with kindness and indulging in self-care activities is a wonderful way to celebrate progress.

Engage in activities that bring you joy and make you feel nurtured. It could be treating yourself to a spa day, going for a nature walk, or indulging in a favorite hobby.

By engaging in self-care, you send a powerful message to yourself that you are deserving of love and care.

Remember, healing from narcissistic abuse is a transformative and ongoing process.

Celebrating progress not only reinforces your self-esteem and confidence but also serves as a reminder of your resilience and strength.

Each step forward, no matter how small, brings you closer to a life filled with self-empowerment and authenticity.

In Chapter 10, we encourage you to celebrate your progress, honor your growth, and acknowledge the strength it takes to heal from narcissistic abuse.

By embracing and celebrating your achievements, you cultivate a positive and empowering mindset, paving the way for a future filled with self-esteem and confidence.

Together, let us embark on this chapter of celebration, as we recognize and honor our progress, no matter how small, and revel in the strength and resilience that lies within each one of us.

Chapter 11: Establishing Healthy Relationships

Learning from Past Experiences: Reflecting on the lessons learned from the abusive relationship and using them as a guide to establishing healthier dynamics in future relationships.

Welcome to Chapter 11, a chapter dedicated to the pursuit of healthy relationships after navigating the challenging terrain of narcissistic abuse.

In this chapter, we will delve into the empowering strategy of learning from past experiences, reflecting on the lessons we have learned from the abusive relationship, and using them as a guide to establish healthier dynamics in future relationships.

One of the most powerful tools we possess on our healing journey is self-reflection.

Taking the time to introspect and understand the dynamics of the abusive relationship can provide invaluable insights into our own vulnerabilities and the red flags we may have overlooked.

By examining the patterns, behaviors, and manipulation tactics employed by the narcissist, we can identify the warning signs and develop a heightened sense of awareness.

Through self-reflection, we gain a deep understanding of our own needs, boundaries, and values.

This self-awareness becomes the foundation for establishing healthier dynamics in future relationships.

It allows us to recognize and prioritize our own well-being, ensuring that we do not compromise our boundaries or sacrifice our authenticity for the sake of others.

Moreover, learning from past experiences helps us develop a stronger sense of discernment.

We become more attuned to the qualities and characteristics that are essential for healthy relationships.

We learn to recognize and appreciate genuine empathy, mutual respect, and open communication as crucial elements in fostering a nourishing and supportive connection.

It is important to note that the lessons we learn from past experiences are not meant to instill fear or skepticism towards all future relationships.

Instead, they serve as guideposts, helping us navigate the complexities of human connection with wisdom and discernment.

By reflecting on our experiences, we become better equipped to set healthy boundaries, communicate our needs effectively, and choose partners who align with our values.

Furthermore, seeking professional guidance, such as therapy or counseling, can provide additional support in the process of establishing healthy relationships.

A trained therapist can assist in uncovering any deep-rooted beliefs or patterns that may hinder our ability to form nourishing connections.

They can guide us in developing effective communication skills and provide tools to navigate potential challenges.

As we embark on the journey of establishing healthy relationships, it is important to approach it with a combination of self-reflection, self-awareness, and self-compassion.

We must remember that healing is a gradual process, and each step we take towards establishing healthier dynamics is a significant achievement.

In Chapter 11, we invite you to reflect on the lessons learned from your past experiences and use them as a compass to guide you towards establishing healthy relationships.

By integrating the wisdom gained from your journey, you have the power to create connections that nurture your well-being, honor your boundaries, and allow for authentic growth and love.

Together, let us embrace the opportunity to forge new paths and cultivate relationships that celebrate our worth, foster growth, and provide a sanctuary of love and support.

Red Flags to Watch Out For: Educating readers on common red flags and warning signs of toxic individuals to avoid repeating patterns of abuse.

Welcome to Chapter 11, where we dive into the crucial topic of establishing healthy relationships after surviving narcissistic abuse.

In this chapter, we will explore an empowering strategy that focuses on recognizing red flags and warning signs of toxic individuals.

By educating ourselves about these indicators, we can protect ourselves from falling into similar patterns of abuse and ensure a healthier future.

One of the key aspects of breaking the cycle of abuse is being able to identify red flags early on in a relationship.

By familiarizing ourselves with the common warning signs exhibited by toxic individuals, we can arm ourselves with knowledge and make informed decisions when it comes to forming new connections.

One important red flag to watch out for is a lack of empathy.

Narcissistic individuals often lack the ability to truly understand and empathize with others.

They may display a lack of concern for the feelings and needs of those around them, focusing solely on their own desires and agenda.

This can manifest as an inability to listen attentively, dismissive behavior, or a pattern of manipulating others for personal gain.

Another red flag is a sense of entitlement.

Toxic individuals with narcissistic traits often have an inflated sense of self-importance and believe they deserve special treatment or privileges.

They may display arrogance, a constant need for admiration, and a tendency to exploit others for their own benefit.

This entitlement can lead to a disregard for boundaries and a tendency to manipulate or control those around them.

Additionally, pay attention to patterns of gaslighting.

Gaslighting is a manipulative tactic used by narcissists to distort your perception of reality and undermine your confidence.

They may deny their own behavior, invalidate your feelings and experiences, or twist the truth to make you doubt your own sanity.

Recognizing these gaslighting techniques can help you maintain clarity and protect your mental and emotional well-being.

Other red flags to be aware of include a lack of accountability, a tendency to belittle or demean others, excessive need for control, and a history of unstable relationships.

It is important to note that these red flags should not be used as a checklist to judge every person we meet, but rather as tools to evaluate behaviors and make informed decisions about our boundaries and well-being.

By understanding and being vigilant about these red flags, we can actively avoid repeating patterns of abuse and create a healthier future for ourselves.

Remember, healing is a process, and establishing healthy relationships takes time and effort.

It is essential to prioritize self-care, trust your instincts, and seek support from trusted friends, family, or professionals along the way.

In Chapter 11, we invite you to educate yourself on the red flags and warning signs of toxic individuals.

By being knowledgeable and discerning, you can navigate the dating scene with confidence and protect yourself from falling into destructive patterns.

Your well-being and happiness are of utmost importance, and by arming yourself with this understanding, you are taking an empowering step towards building the healthy, loving relationships you deserve.

Together, let us embrace the journey of establishing healthy relationships, free from the grip of narcissistic abuse.

By recognizing the red flags and honoring our boundaries, we can create a future filled with genuine connections, mutual respect, and a renewed sense of self-worth.

Boundaries in Relationships: Providing guidance on establishing and maintaining healthy boundaries in all types of relationships.

Welcome to Chapter 11, where we delve into the essential topic of boundaries in relationships.

This empowering strategy focuses on providing guidance to help you establish and maintain healthy boundaries in all types of relationships.

By understanding the importance of boundaries and implementing effective strategies, you can navigate relationships with confidence and protect yourself from the harmful effects of narcissistic abuse.

Boundaries serve as a crucial framework for healthy relationships.

They define the limits of what is acceptable and unacceptable behavior, ensuring that your needs, values, and well-being are respected.

Establishing and communicating boundaries is a fundamental aspect of self-care and self-respect, allowing you to maintain your sense of identity and protect yourself from manipulation and exploitation.

One key aspect of setting boundaries is identifying your personal values and needs.

Take the time to reflect on what matters most to you in relationships and what you require to feel safe, respected, and fulfilled.

This self-reflection will serve as a foundation for establishing boundaries that align with your values and promote your overall well-being.

It is important to remember that boundaries are not rigid walls but flexible guidelines that can adapt to different situations and relationships.

They are designed to foster open communication, mutual respect, and healthy interactions.

By setting clear and assertive boundaries, you create an environment where your needs are heard, understood, and honored.

When establishing boundaries, it is essential to communicate them effectively.

Clearly and assertively express your boundaries to others, making sure they understand your expectations and limitations.

Use "I" statements to express your needs and feelings, and be specific about what behavior is acceptable and what is not.

Effective communication of boundaries sets the tone for healthy interactions and promotes understanding and respect between individuals.

Maintaining boundaries requires consistency and self-awareness.

Be vigilant about enforcing your boundaries and assertively addressing any violations.

Remember that boundaries are not meant to please others but to protect your well-being.

It is normal for others to test your boundaries, especially if they have been used to crossing them in the past.

Stay firm in upholding your boundaries and be prepared to take appropriate action if necessary.

In addition to establishing and maintaining personal boundaries, it is equally important to respect the boundaries of others.

By practicing reciprocity, you create a healthy dynamic that values mutual respect and consideration.

Respecting the boundaries of others fosters trust, enhances communication, and cultivates healthier relationships overall.

Navigating relationships after experiencing narcissistic abuse can be challenging, but by establishing and maintaining healthy boundaries, you are taking a powerful step towards healing and reclaiming your personal power.

Boundaries serve as a compass, guiding you towards relationships that are built on trust, respect, and genuine connection.

In Chapter 11, we invite you to explore the art of setting boundaries in relationships.

By understanding their significance, identifying your needs and values, effectively communicating your boundaries, and practicing reciprocity, you can create a foundation for healthy and fulfilling connections.

Remember, setting boundaries is an ongoing process that requires self-awareness, self-care, and a commitment to your well-being.

Together, let us embark on this journey of establishing healthy relationships, where boundaries become the pillars that safeguard your happiness and empower you to build the authentic connections you deserve.

Building Trust: Exploring strategies to rebuild trust in oneself and others after experiencing betrayal and manipulation.

I n Chapter 11, we dive into the crucial topic of building trust in oneself and others after experiencing betrayal and manipulation.

Rebuilding trust is a significant step in establishing healthy relationships following narcissistic abuse.

This empowering strategy explores various strategies to regain trust and restore faith in oneself and others.

Experiencing narcissistic abuse can shatter our ability to trust.

It leaves us questioning our own judgment and doubting the intentions of others.

However, it is important to remember that trust can be rebuilt with time, self-reflection, and intentional effort.

To begin the process of rebuilding trust, it is essential to focus on self-trust.

Start by acknowledging your own resilience and strength in overcoming the challenges you have faced.

Engage in self-reflection to gain a deeper understanding of the patterns and vulnerabilities that led to the abusive relationship.

By learning from past experiences, you can develop a stronger sense of self-awareness and make informed decisions moving forward.

Practicing self-compassion is also paramount in rebuilding trust.

Show yourself kindness and understanding as you navigate the healing journey.

Recognize that the abuse was not your fault and allow yourself the space to heal and grow.

By practicing self-compassion, you can cultivate a positive self-image and enhance your ability to trust in your own judgment.

Rebuilding trust in others requires a gradual and discerning approach.

It is important to surround yourself with supportive and trustworthy individuals who respect your boundaries and prioritize your well-being.

Take the time to observe their actions and consistency, allowing trust to develop naturally over time.

Engaging in open and honest communication is vital when rebuilding trust in relationships.

Express your feelings and concerns in a clear and assertive manner, while also being open to listening to the perspectives of others.

Effective communication promotes understanding, transparency, and the opportunity for healing in relationships.

Forgiveness is an integral part of the trust-building process.

While forgiveness does not mean forgetting or condoning the actions of the narcissistic abuser, it does mean releasing the emotional burden and resentment that may be holding you back.

Forgiveness is a personal choice that allows you to move forward with a lighter heart and an open mind.

As you work towards rebuilding trust, remember to honor your intuition.

Trust your instincts and be mindful of any red flags or warning signs that may arise in new relationships.

Your intuition serves as a valuable guide and protector, helping you make informed decisions and maintain your boundaries.

Rebuilding trust is a journey that requires patience, self-reflection, and the willingness to take risks.

It may not happen overnight, but with time and consistent effort, you can restore your faith in yourself and others.

Surround yourself with a supportive network, engage in self-care practices, and remain committed to your personal growth.

Chapter 11 invites you to explore the empowering strategies for building trust after experiencing narcissistic abuse.

By focusing on self-trust, practicing self-compassion, engaging in open communication, embracing forgiveness, and honoring your intuition, you can lay the foundation for healthier and more fulfilling relationships.

Remember, trust is a precious gift that can be rebuilt, allowing you to embrace the joys and connections that life has to offer.

Together, let us embark on the journey of rebuilding trust and establishing healthy relationships, where trust becomes the bridge that connects us to genuine connections, love, and healing.

Chapter 12: Forgiveness and Moving On

Understanding Forgiveness: Addressing the misconceptions around forgiveness and emphasizing that forgiveness is a personal choice, separate from reconciliation.

In Chapter 12, we delve into the complex topic of forgiveness and its role in the healing process after narcissistic abuse.

It is essential to understand that forgiveness is a personal choice and should not be confused with reconciliation.

Let us address the misconceptions surrounding forgiveness and explore its profound significance in our journey towards healing and moving forward.

Forgiveness is often misunderstood as condoning or forgetting the abusive actions inflicted upon us.

However, forgiveness is a deeply personal and empowering decision that we make for ourselves, not for the abuser.

It is a choice to release the anger, resentment, and pain that may be holding us back from fully embracing our future.

One of the misconceptions surrounding forgiveness is that it requires us to reconcile with the narcissistic abuser or to forget the past.

However, forgiveness does not necessitate a reunion or a continuation of the abusive relationship.

It is about freeing ourselves from the emotional burden that prevents us from living a fulfilled and joyful life.

Forgiveness is a process that varies from person to person.

It is not something that can be rushed or forced.

It may take time and self-reflection to arrive at a place where forgiveness feels authentic and genuine.

It is important to honor our own healing journey and give ourselves the space and patience needed to navigate this complex terrain.

Forgiveness does not mean that we minimize or dismiss the impact of the abuse we endured.

It is a conscious choice to let go of the negative emotions and reclaim our power and inner peace.

It allows us to break free from the chains of resentment and bitterness, and to focus our energy on rebuilding our lives.

It is important to recognize that forgiveness is not a linear process.

There may be moments of anger, sadness, and frustration along the way.

It is natural to experience a range of emotions as we navigate the path towards forgiveness.

By acknowledging and allowing ourselves to feel these emotions, we can move closer to a place of healing and acceptance.

Forgiveness also involves extending compassion towards ourselves.

It means embracing our vulnerabilities and recognizing that we are not defined by the abuse we experienced.

Self-compassion allows us to acknowledge our own pain, validate our emotions, and nurture ourselves with kindness and understanding.

Moving on from narcissistic abuse is a journey that intertwines with the process of forgiveness.

As we release the grip of resentment and anger, we create space for new beginnings and a renewed sense of self.

It is a journey of self-discovery, personal growth, and the reclamation of our power and autonomy.

In Chapter 12, we explore the profound impact of forgiveness and its integral role in our healing process.

By understanding the true nature of forgiveness as a personal choice separate from reconciliation, we empower ourselves to let go of the past and embrace a brighter future.

Through self-compassion, patience, and a commitment to our own well-being, we can forge a path towards forgiveness and the freedom it brings.

Let us embark on this transformative chapter of forgiveness and moving on, where we release the weight of the past and embrace the possibility of a life filled with peace, joy, and genuine connections.

Together, we will navigate the intricacies of forgiveness and forge a new path towards healing and wholeness.

Letting Go of Resentment and Anger: Offering forgiveness exercises and techniques to release resentment and anger, promoting emotional healing and personal freedom.

In Chapter 12, we dive into the profound topic of forgiveness and its transformative power in the journey of healing from narcissistic abuse.

In this chapter, we focus on one crucial aspect of forgiveness: letting go of resentment and anger.

By offering forgiveness exercises and techniques, we aim to guide you towards releasing these toxic emotions, facilitating emotional healing, and reclaiming your personal freedom.

Resentment and anger are natural responses to the pain and betrayal caused by narcissistic abuse.

However, holding onto these emotions can hinder our ability to move forward and experience true healing.

It is essential to recognize that forgiveness is not about denying or minimizing the harm inflicted upon us, but rather about freeing ourselves from the emotional burdens that keep us trapped in the past.

To begin the process of letting go of resentment and anger, it is important to acknowledge and validate your emotions.

Take the time to reflect on the specific incidents that caused you pain and the subsequent feelings that arose within you.

By journaling or engaging in therapeutic practices, you can give voice to your emotions and gain a deeper understanding of their origins.

One effective forgiveness exercise involves writing a letter to the person who caused you harm.

This is a personal and cathartic practice that allows you to express your emotions, confront the pain, and ultimately release it.

It is crucial to remember that this letter is for your eyes only.

It is an opportunity to articulate your feelings honestly and authentically, without the need for confrontation or reconciliation.

Another technique to let go of resentment and anger is through mindfulness and meditation.

By practicing present-moment awareness, you can observe your emotions without judgment and create space for healing.

Mindfulness helps you cultivate compassion for yourself and others, fostering a sense of empathy that contributes to the forgiveness process.

Self-care plays a significant role in releasing resentment and anger.

Engaging in activities that bring you joy, relaxation, and fulfillment helps redirect your focus from negative emotions to self-nurturing.

This might involve engaging in hobbies, spending time in nature, seeking support from loved ones, or seeking professional guidance through therapy or counseling.

It is important to acknowledge that letting go of resentment and anger is a journey that takes time and effort.

It is a deeply personal process, and the timeline for forgiveness will vary for each individual.

Be patient and compassionate with yourself as you navigate the complexities of healing.

By embracing forgiveness and letting go of resentment and anger, you open up space for emotional healing and personal freedom.

142

You reclaim your power and take control of your narrative, no longer allowing the past to define your present or dictate your future.

Remember, forgiveness is a gift you give yourself—an act of self-liberation and an opportunity to create a brighter and more fulfilling life.

In Chapter 12, we explore the power of forgiveness and guide you through exercises and techniques to release resentment and anger.

By incorporating these empowering strategies into your healing journey, you can cultivate emotional well-being, reclaim your personal freedom, and create a life filled with joy, authenticity, and genuine connections.

Let us embark on this transformative chapter of forgiveness and moving on, where we let go of the weight of resentment and anger and embrace the possibility of a life filled with peace, healing, and emotional liberation.

Together, we will navigate the intricacies of forgiveness and forge a new path towards healing and wholeness.

Focusing on Personal Growth: Encouraging readers to shift their focus from the past to the present and future, embracing personal growth opportunities and creating a fulfilling life.

Welcome to Chapter 12, where we delve into the profound concepts of forgiveness and moving on as crucial components of healing from narcissistic abuse.

In this chapter, we emphasize the importance of focusing on personal growth and redirecting our attention from the past to the present and future.

By embracing personal growth opportunities, we can create a fulfilling and meaningful life beyond the confines of the abusive relationship.

When we experience narcissistic abuse, it is natural to get caught up in the pain and trauma of the past.

However, dwelling on the past can hinder our progress and prevent us from fully embracing the possibilities that lie ahead.

By shifting our focus to the present and future, we open ourselves up to a world of personal growth and self-discovery.

One powerful way to focus on personal growth is by setting meaningful goals for yourself.

These goals can be both short-term and long-term, encompassing various aspects of your life, such as career, relationships, health, and personal development.

Setting goals gives you a sense of purpose and direction, providing a roadmap for your journey of personal growth.

In addition to goal-setting, it is important to engage in continuous learning and self-improvement.

This can involve seeking out educational opportunities, attending workshops or seminars, reading self-help books, or even enlisting the support of a mentor or coach.

By actively seeking knowledge and growth, you expand your horizons and unlock your full potential.

Embracing personal growth also means nurturing your physical, emotional, and spiritual well-being.

Engage in self-care practices that replenish your energy and promote overall wellness.

This might include activities such as exercise, meditation, practicing mindfulness, spending time in nature, or pursuing creative outlets that bring you joy and fulfillment.

It is crucial to remember that personal growth is not a linear process.

It involves embracing both successes and setbacks, learning from challenges, and adapting along the way.

Give yourself permission to make mistakes and view them as opportunities for growth and learning.

Embrace resilience and perseverance as you navigate the path of personal growth.

As you focus on personal growth, it is essential to surround yourself with a supportive network of friends, family, and like-minded individuals.

Seek out communities or support groups where you can share experiences, gain insights, and receive encouragement.

Connecting with others who have undergone similar experiences can be empowering and validating.

Ultimately, the journey of personal growth is about discovering and embracing your authentic self.

It is about realizing your worth, embracing your strengths, and letting go of the limitations imposed by the narcissistic abuse.

As you embark on this journey, remember that you have the power to create a fulfilling and meaningful life beyond the scars of the past.

In Chapter 12, we explore the transformative power of focusing on personal growth and shifting our attention to the present and future.

By incorporating these empowering strategies into your healing journey, you can embark on a path of self-discovery, resilience, and personal fulfillment.

Together, we will navigate the intricacies of forgiveness and moving on, forging a new path towards a life that celebrates personal growth and embraces the limitless possibilities that lie ahead.

Join us as we delve into Chapter 12, where we unlock the secrets to personal growth, resilience, and the creation of a life filled with purpose, joy, and authentic self-expression.

Let us embrace the power of focusing on personal growth as we heal, reclaim our lives, and step into a brighter future filled with endless opportunities for growth and fulfillment.

Embracing New Beginnings: Inspiring readers to embrace the journey of moving on, letting go of the past, and embracing new opportunities and relationships.

Welcome to Chapter 12, where we explore the transformative power of embracing new beginnings after narcissistic abuse.

In this chapter, we inspire readers to let go of the past and open themselves up to new opportunities and relationships.

Moving on from the pain and trauma of narcissistic abuse is a courageous and empowering journey, and it begins with embracing the notion of new beginnings.

One of the first steps in embracing new beginnings is to acknowledge and accept the past for what it was.

It is essential to allow yourself the space and time to heal from the wounds inflicted by narcissistic abuse.

This may involve seeking professional help, such as therapy or counseling, to process your emotions and gain clarity on the impact of the abuse.

As you heal, it's important to shift your mindset and focus on the present and future.

This means reframing your perspective and embracing a positive outlook.

Understand that the abuse you experienced does not define your worth or dictate your future.

You have the power to create a new narrative for yourself, one that is filled with hope, resilience, and personal growth.

Embracing new beginnings also involves letting go of any lingering resentment, anger, or blame towards the narcissistic abuser.

It's a process of freeing yourself from the emotional burden and reclaiming your power.

Forgiveness, in this context, is not about condoning or forgetting the abuse, but about liberating yourself from the grip of negativity and allowing yourself to move forward.

In addition to letting go, it's important to open yourself up to new opportunities and relationships.

This may involve taking calculated risks, stepping outside of your comfort zone, and exploring new interests or passions.

Embrace the excitement and possibilities that come with embarking on a new journey.

Surround yourself with positive influences and seek out relationships that are built on trust, respect, and mutual support.

As you embrace new beginnings, remember to be patient and kind to yourself.

Healing and moving on takes time and may involve setbacks along the way. It's important to practice self-compassion and celebrate small victories.

Every step forward, no matter how small, is a testament to your strength and resilience.

In conclusion, Chapter 12 delves into the empowering concept of embracing new beginnings after narcissistic abuse.

By letting go of the past, reframing your perspective, and opening yourself up to new opportunities and relationships, you can embark on a journey of personal growth, healing, and empowerment.

Embrace the power of new beginnings as you step into a future filled with hope, self-discovery, and the realization of your true potential.

Join us in Chapter 12 as we explore the intricacies of embracing new beginnings and learn how to navigate the path of healing, resilience, and personal fulfillment.

Let go of the past, embrace the present, and step into a future filled with endless possibilities.

Together, we will empower ourselves to create a life that is defined by our strength, authenticity, and unwavering commitment to personal growth.

Chapter 13: Parenting After Narcissistic Abuse

Protecting Children from Narcissistic Parents: Providing guidance on how to shield children from the negative influence of a narcissistic parent and create a safe and nurturing environment.

Welcome to Chapter 13, where we delve into the important topic of parenting after narcissistic abuse.

This chapter provides valuable guidance on how to protect children from the negative influence of a narcissistic parent and create a safe and nurturing environment for their growth and development.

Navigating parenting in the aftermath of narcissistic abuse can be challenging, but with the right strategies and support, it is possible to provide children with the love, stability, and security they deserve.

One of the key aspects of protecting children from narcissistic parents is to establish clear boundaries and maintain consistent rules and expectations.

Narcissistic parents often lack empathy and may prioritize their own needs and desires above their children's well-being.

By setting firm boundaries and maintaining a predictable environment, you create a sense of stability and safety for your children.

This includes clearly defining appropriate behavior, consequences for misbehavior, and promoting open communication within the family.

It's crucial to shield children from the emotional manipulation and gaslighting techniques often employed by narcissistic parents.

Educating yourself about narcissistic abuse and its impact on children is essential.

Recognizing the signs of manipulation and gaslighting can help you intervene and protect your children from psychological harm.

Encourage open dialogue with your children, create a safe space for them to express their feelings, and validate their experiences.

In addition to protecting children from the negative influence of a narcissistic parent, it is important to foster their self-esteem and self-worth.

Narcissistic abuse can leave children feeling invalidated, unworthy, and insecure.

By providing them with unconditional love, positive reinforcement, and opportunities for personal growth, you can help them develop a strong sense of self.

Encourage their interests, celebrate their achievements, and emphasize their unique qualities and strengths.

Seeking professional help, such as therapy or counseling, can be instrumental in supporting both you and your children through the healing process.

A qualified therapist can provide guidance, validation, and coping strategies tailored to your specific situation.

They can also help you navigate co-parenting challenges and develop effective strategies for communication and conflict resolution.

Remember, healing from narcissistic abuse is a journey that requires time, patience, and support.

It is important to prioritize self-care and seek help when needed.

Building a strong support system, whether through trusted friends, support groups, or online communities, can provide you with the encouragement and understanding you need as you navigate the complexities of parenting after narcissistic abuse.

In conclusion, Chapter 13 addresses the vital topic of parenting after narcissistic abuse.

By implementing strategies to protect children from the negative influence of a narcissistic parent, fostering their self-esteem, and seeking professional help, you can create a safe and nurturing environment for their growth and development.

Together, we will empower ourselves to break the cycle of abuse, provide our children with the love and support they deserve, and create a future filled with resilience, healing, and genuine connection.

Join us in Chapter 13 as we explore the complexities of parenting after narcissistic abuse and learn how to navigate the path of protecting and empowering our children.

Together, we will create a safe haven where our children can thrive, grow, and flourish despite the challenges they may have faced.

Co-Parenting Strategies: Offering effective co-parenting techniques, including parallel parenting and clear communication, to minimize conflict and prioritize the child's well-being.

Welcome to Chapter 13, where we dive into the crucial topic of parenting after narcissistic abuse.

This chapter provides invaluable guidance on co-parenting strategies to help you navigate the complexities of raising children with a narcissistic ex-partner.

By implementing effective co-parenting techniques, such as parallel parenting and clear communication, you can minimize conflict and prioritize your child's well-being.

Co-parenting with a narcissistic ex-partner can be challenging, as they may seek to maintain control and manipulate the dynamics of the relationship.

Parallel parenting is a strategy that allows each parent to have minimal direct contact and make decisions independently, reducing opportunities for conflict.

This approach enables you to focus on your child's needs and maintain consistency in parenting, while minimizing opportunities for your ex-partner to engage in power struggles or attempts to undermine your authority.

Clear communication is essential when co-parenting after narcissistic abuse.

It's important to establish a communication plan that sets boundaries and guidelines for interactions.

This may include using written communication, such as email or a dedicated co-parenting app, to ensure documentation and accountability.

By keeping communication focused on child-related matters and avoiding personal attacks or manipulation, you can maintain a more peaceful co-parenting environment.

When co-parenting with a narcissistic ex-partner, it's crucial to prioritize your child's well-being above all else.

Focus on creating a stable and nurturing environment for your child, free from the emotional turmoil and manipulation that may have been present during the abusive relationship.

Establish consistent routines and rules that provide a sense of security and predictability for your child.

Educating yourself about narcissistic personality disorder and its impact on children can be instrumental in understanding your child's experiences and providing appropriate support.

Recognize the potential effects of the abuse on your child's emotional well-being and self-esteem, and be proactive in addressing their needs.

Encourage open communication with your child, validate their feelings, and provide them with the space to express themselves without fear of judgment or retaliation.

Seeking professional help, such as therapy or counseling, for both you and your child can be immensely beneficial.

A qualified therapist can guide you in navigating the challenges of co-parenting after narcissistic abuse, help you develop effective coping strategies, and provide support for your child's healing journey.

They can also assist in addressing any residual trauma or emotional wounds that may impact your child's development.

Remember, co-parenting after narcissistic abuse requires strength, patience, and a focus on the well-being of your child.

It's important to practice self-care, set boundaries with your ex-partner, and surround yourself with a strong support network.

By prioritizing your child's needs, implementing effective co-parenting strategies, and seeking professional help when necessary, you can create a nurturing environment that allows your child to thrive despite the challenges they may have faced.

In conclusion, Chapter 13 addresses the complex topic of parenting after narcissistic abuse and offers strategies to promote effective co-parenting.

By implementing parallel parenting and clear communication techniques, prioritizing your child's well-being, and seeking professional help, you can create a supportive and stable environment for your child's growth and development.

Together, we can empower ourselves as parents, break the cycle of abuse, and provide our children with the love and care they deserve.

Join us in Chapter 13 as we explore the intricacies of co-parenting after narcissistic abuse and learn how to navigate this challenging journey with resilience, empathy, and a steadfast commitment to our children's well-being.

Together, we can create a brighter future for our families, built on trust, healthy communication, and the unconditional love that our children deserve.

Helping Children Heal: Providing age-appropriate resources and support to help children heal from the effects of narcissistic abuse and develop healthy relationships.

Welcome to Chapter 13, where we delve into the essential topic of parenting after narcissistic abuse.

In this chapter, we provide valuable insights into helping children heal from the effects of narcissistic abuse and empower them to develop healthy relationships.

We understand the profound impact that narcissistic abuse can have on children, and we are here to offer age-appropriate resources and support to aid in their healing process.

Children who have experienced narcissistic abuse may carry emotional scars that require careful attention and nurturing.

It is crucial to provide them with a safe and supportive environment where they can process their emotions and begin their healing journey.

Age-appropriate resources, such as books, articles, and therapeutic activities, can play a vital role in helping children understand their experiences and develop healthy coping mechanisms.

One important aspect of supporting children in healing from narcissistic abuse is validating their feelings and experiences.

Children may have been subjected to manipulation, gaslighting, or emotional neglect, which can leave them questioning their own reality.

By actively listening to their concerns, providing empathy, and assuring them that their feelings are valid, we can help restore their sense of self-worth and trust in their own perceptions.

It is crucial to equip children with the knowledge and skills necessary to establish healthy relationships in the future.

Teaching them about boundaries, consent, and healthy communication can empower them to recognize and avoid toxic dynamics.

Introducing these concepts in age-appropriate ways, such as through storytelling or role-playing exercises, can make them more accessible and engaging for children.

In addition to providing emotional support, it is important to involve professionals, such as therapists or counselors, who specialize in working with children who have experienced narcissistic abuse.

These experts can offer tailored interventions and therapeutic techniques to help children process their trauma, develop resilience, and build healthy relationship patterns.

Through play therapy, art therapy, or other evidence-based approaches, children can explore their emotions and experiences in a safe and supportive setting.

Parental self-care is also paramount when supporting children in healing from narcissistic abuse.

As parents, we must prioritize our own healing journey and seek support to ensure we are in the best possible emotional state to guide our children.

By engaging in self-care practices, such as therapy, support groups, or activities that bring joy and relaxation, we model healthy coping mechanisms and reinforce the importance of self-care for our children.

It is worth noting that each child's healing journey is unique, and the pace at which they heal may vary.

Patience, compassion, and understanding are key as we support our children through this process.

By providing a loving and nurturing environment, accessing appropriate resources and professional help, and fostering open and honest communication, we can help our children heal from the effects of narcissistic abuse and develop healthy relationships as they grow.

In conclusion, Chapter 13 focuses on parenting after narcissistic abuse and emphasizes the importance of helping children heal from the trauma they have experienced.

By providing age-appropriate resources, validating their feelings, teaching them about healthy relationships, involving professionals, and prioritizing parental self-care, we can support our children on their healing journey.

Together, we can empower them to break free from the cycle of abuse, cultivate resilience, and build a future filled with love, respect, and healthy connections.

Join us in Chapter 13 as we explore the empowering strategies to help children heal from narcissistic abuse and guide them towards developing healthy relationships.

Together, we can create a nurturing environment where our children thrive, overcome their past, and embrace a future filled with happiness, love, and resilience.

Chapter 14: Thriving After Narcissistic Abuse

Celebrating Progress and Personal Victories: Encouraging readers to celebrate their milestones, resilience, and personal growth as they transition from surviving to thriving.

Welcome to Chapter 14, where we explore the transformative journey of thriving after narcissistic abuse.

In this chapter, we invite readers to celebrate their progress, personal victories, and resilience as they transition from surviving to thriving.

We understand the tremendous strength and courage it takes to overcome the effects of narcissistic abuse, and we are here to support and empower you on this remarkable path of healing and growth.

One of the most empowering aspects of healing from narcissistic abuse is acknowledging and celebrating your milestones.

Each step forward, no matter how small, is a testament to your strength and determination.

It's important to recognize and appreciate the progress you have made along the way.

Take the time to reflect on the personal growth you have achieved, the boundaries you have set, and the self-care practices you have embraced.

Celebrating these victories reinforces your resilience and reinforces the positive changes you have made in your life.

As you transition from surviving to thriving, it's important to redefine your sense of self-worth and reclaim your personal power.

The journey of healing allows you to rediscover your authentic self and embrace your unique strengths and abilities.

Recognize that you are not defined by the abuse you have experienced, but rather by your resilience, courage, and capacity for growth.

Celebrate the newfound sense of self and the liberation that comes with reclaiming your personal power.

Thriving after narcissistic abuse also involves cultivating a positive and empowering mindset.

Challenge the negative beliefs and self-doubt instilled by the narcissist and replace them with affirming and empowering self-perceptions.

Embrace self-compassion and practice self-love, recognizing that you deserve happiness, love, and fulfillment.

Celebrate the moments when you show yourself kindness, forgiveness, and acceptance.

These acts of self-compassion are pivotal in nurturing your emotional well-being and creating a foundation for thriving.

Building a strong support network is crucial as you continue to thrive after narcissistic abuse.

Surround yourself with understanding and compassionate individuals who uplift and validate your experiences.

Seek out support groups, therapy, or online communities where you can connect with others who have gone through similar journeys.

Celebrate the connections you make, the shared wisdom, and the strength that comes from knowing you are not alone in your experiences.

Thriving after narcissistic abuse also involves pursuing your passions and finding joy in life.

Reconnect with the activities, hobbies, and interests that bring you fulfillment.

Celebrate the moments when you engage in self-care and prioritize your own happiness.

Embrace the opportunities to explore new experiences, set meaningful goals, and create a life that aligns with your values and aspirations.

Celebrating these moments of joy and personal fulfillment reinforces your capacity for happiness and reminds you that you are deserving of a life that brings you genuine happiness.

In conclusion, Chapter 14 focuses on thriving after narcissistic abuse and encourages readers to celebrate their progress, personal victories, and resilience.

By acknowledging and appreciating your milestones, reclaiming your personal power, cultivating a positive mindset, building a support network, and pursuing joy and fulfillment, you can embark on a journey of thriving.

Celebrate your strength, growth, and capacity for happiness as you create a life that goes beyond surviving and truly embraces the joy of thriving.

Join us in Chapter 14 as we explore the empowering strategies to celebrate your progress and personal victories as you transition from surviving to thriving after narcissistic abuse.

Together, we will honor your resilience, cultivate self-compassion, and create a life filled with joy, fulfillment, and authentic happiness.

Cultivating Resilience: Introducing resilience-building practices, such as positive affirmations, gratitude, and embracing challenges as opportunities for growth.

Welcome to Chapter 14, where we dive into the transformative journey of thriving after narcissistic abuse.

In this chapter, we will explore the empowering strategies to cultivate resilience, allowing you to overcome the challenges you have faced and embrace a life filled with strength, growth, and fulfillment.

Cultivating resilience is a vital aspect of healing and thriving after narcissistic abuse.

It involves developing the inner strength and capacity to bounce back from adversity, reclaim your power, and create a life that aligns with your true self.

In this chapter, we introduce various resilience-building practices that can support you on this journey.

One powerful technique is the use of positive affirmations.

These are statements that reflect your strengths, worthiness, and potential. By repeating affirmations such as "I am strong," "I am worthy of love," and "I have the power to create a positive future," you can rewire your mindset and replace the negative beliefs instilled by the narcissistic abuse.

Celebrate the moments when you embrace positive affirmations and recognize the transformative impact they have on your self-perception and resilience.

Gratitude is another essential practice in cultivating resilience.

By focusing on the things you are grateful for, even in the midst of challenging times, you shift your perspective and invite more positivity into your life.

Take a moment each day to reflect on the moments, people, or things you appreciate.

Celebrate the moments when you embrace gratitude and witness the profound impact it has on your overall well-being and ability to navigate adversity.

Embracing challenges as opportunities for growth is a mindset shift that empowers you to see difficulties as stepping stones to resilience and personal development.

Rather than viewing obstacles as insurmountable barriers, celebrate the moments when you approach challenges with a growth-oriented mindset.

Recognize that every hurdle you overcome strengthens your resilience, builds your confidence, and contributes to your ability to thrive.

In addition to these practices, it's important to surround yourself with supportive and understanding individuals who can bolster your resilience.

Seek out a therapist, support group, or mentor who can provide guidance, validation, and encouragement on your journey.

Celebrate the connections you make and the support you receive, knowing that you are not alone in your experiences.

Furthermore, cultivating resilience involves taking care of your physical and emotional well-being.

Engage in self-care activities that replenish your energy and nurture your soul.

Celebrate the moments when you prioritize your needs and engage in practices such as exercise, mindfulness, journaling, or engaging in hobbies that bring you joy.

These acts of self-care celebrate your commitment to self-love and reinforce your resilience.

In conclusion, Chapter 14 delves into the empowering strategies to cultivate resilience and thrive after narcissistic abuse.

Through the practices of positive affirmations, gratitude, embracing challenges, building a support network, and engaging in self-care, you can develop the resilience needed to overcome the effects of narcissistic abuse and create a life that is filled with strength, growth, and fulfillment.

Join us in Chapter 14 as we explore the transformative journey of cultivating resilience and thriving after narcissistic abuse.

Celebrate the moments when you embrace resilience-building practices, witness your growth, and unlock the potential within you to create a life that goes beyond surviving and truly embraces the joy of thriving.

Together, we will celebrate your resilience and empower you to reclaim your power and live a life filled with purpose and authenticity.

Embracing Personal Strengths: Assisting readers in identifying their unique strengths and talents, empowering them to build a fulfilling and purposeful life beyond the abuse.

Welcome to Chapter 14, where we embark on the empowering journey of thriving after narcissistic abuse.

In this chapter, we will explore the transformative strategies that will guide you towards embracing your personal strengths, helping you build a fulfilling and purposeful life beyond the shadows of the abuse you have endured.

Identifying and embracing your unique strengths and talents is an essential step towards reclaiming your power and creating a life that aligns with your authentic self.

Many individuals who have experienced narcissistic abuse often struggle with self-doubt and a diminished sense of self-worth.

In this chapter, we will assist you in recognizing your inherent strengths and abilities, empowering you to move forward with confidence and purpose.

One powerful technique for discovering your personal strengths is through self-reflection and introspection.

Take the time to explore your interests, passions, and natural abilities.

What activities or subjects bring you joy and fulfillment?

What skills or talents have others recognized in you?

By acknowledging these areas of strength, you can tap into your potential and cultivate a life that allows you to express and thrive in these areas.

Another valuable resource for identifying personal strengths is seeking feedback from trusted individuals in your life.

Reach out to supportive friends, family members, or mentors and ask them to share their observations about your strengths and positive qualities.

Sometimes, others can provide valuable insights that we may not recognize ourselves.

Celebrate the moments when you gather feedback and embrace the newfound knowledge of your strengths.

Furthermore, it is important to understand that personal strengths are not limited to specific talents or skills.

They also encompass inner qualities such as resilience, empathy, determination, and adaptability.

Celebrate the moments when you recognize these traits within yourself and acknowledge the profound impact they have on your journey towards healing and growth.

Once you have identified your personal strengths, it is time to integrate them into your daily life and pursue activities and goals that align with them.

Celebrate the moments when you actively seek opportunities that allow you to showcase your strengths and engage in activities that bring you a sense of purpose and fulfillment.

By harnessing your strengths, you are laying the foundation for a life that is driven by your unique qualities and passions.

Additionally, don't be afraid to seek professional guidance to further explore and develop your strengths.

Working with a coach or therapist who specializes in narcissistic abuse recovery can provide invaluable support and guidance as you navigate the path of healing and thriving.

Celebrate the moments when you prioritize your personal growth and invest in your well-being.

In conclusion, Chapter 14 invites you to embrace your personal strengths as a catalyst for building a fulfilling and purposeful life beyond narcissistic abuse.

By recognizing and harnessing your unique abilities, talents, and inner qualities, you are empowering yourself to reclaim your power, overcome the effects of abuse, and create a future that is rooted in authenticity and personal fulfillment.

Join us in Chapter 14 as we delve into the transformative journey of embracing personal strengths.

Celebrate the moments when you uncover your true potential and embark on a path that honors your unique qualities and passions.

Together, we will celebrate your resilience, empower you to reclaim your power, and guide you towards a life of fulfillment, purpose, and self-empowerment.

Pursuing Passion and Purpose: Guiding readers in exploring their passions and finding meaning and purpose in their lives, allowing them to thrive and create a life of fulfillment.

Welcome to Chapter 14, where we embark on a transformative journey towards thriving after narcissistic abuse.

In this chapter, we will delve into the empowering strategies that will guide you in pursuing your passions and finding meaning and purpose in your life.

By embracing your passions and aligning your life with your true purpose, you can unlock a world of fulfillment and create a life that goes beyond mere survival.

One of the key elements of thriving after narcissistic abuse is reconnecting with your passions.

Often, during the abusive relationship, your passions may have been suppressed or neglected.

Now is the time to explore and rediscover what truly ignites your soul.

Reflect on the activities, hobbies, or interests that have brought you joy and fulfillment in the past.

Celebrate the moments when you dedicate time and energy to reconnect with these passions.

Finding meaning and purpose in your life is a vital step towards thriving.

It involves aligning your actions and goals with your core values and beliefs.

Take the time to reflect on what truly matters to you.

What are your aspirations, dreams, and values? Celebrate the moments when you embrace the pursuit of a purpose-driven life.

To help you in this journey, it can be beneficial to engage in self-exploration exercises and seek inspiration from various sources.

Celebrate the moments when you immerse yourself in books, podcasts, or workshops that explore personal growth and finding meaning in life.

Surround yourself with individuals who inspire you and share similar passions.

Celebrate the moments when you actively seek out new experiences and environments that nurture your growth and fulfillment.

Moreover, consider how your passions and purpose can positively impact others.

Is there a way you can use your talents and interests to make a difference in the lives of others or contribute to a cause you care about? Celebrate the moments when you realize the profound impact your passions can have beyond yourself.

Thriving after narcissistic abuse is not about erasing the past, but about using it as a catalyst for growth and transformation.

Celebrate the moments when you embrace your past experiences and use them as a source of wisdom and strength.

Your journey of healing and empowerment can inspire and support others who have faced similar challenges.

In conclusion, Chapter 14 invites you to pursue your passions and find meaning and purpose in your life as essential components of thriving after narcissistic abuse.

By reconnecting with your passions, aligning your actions with your core values, and using your strengths to make a positive impact, you can create a life of fulfillment and contribute to a better world.

Celebrate the moments when you embark on this empowering journey, embracing your true passions, and finding meaning that allows you to thrive beyond the shadows of abuse.

Join us in Chapter 14 as we explore the path to pursuing passion and purpose.

Celebrate the moments when you immerse yourself in the discovery of your passions, align your actions with your values, and find profound meaning in your life.

Together, we will celebrate your resilience, guide you towards a life of fulfillment, and empower you to thrive beyond the challenges of narcissistic abuse.

Chapter 15: Resources and Support

Additional Reading Materials and Recommended Books: Providing a comprehensive list of books and resources that delve deeper into narcissism, abuse recovery, and personal growth.

Welcome to Chapter 15, where we provide you with a valuable collection of additional reading materials and recommended books to support you on your journey of unmasking narcissism, navigating through abuse, and achieving personal growth.

This comprehensive list of resources has been carefully curated to provide you with insights and knowledge from experts in the field, empowering you with the tools and information you need to heal and thrive.

One of the key aspects of recovering from narcissistic abuse is gaining a deeper understanding of narcissism itself.

We recommend books such as "Disarming the Narcissist" by Wendy T. Behary, which offers practical strategies to disarm narcissistic behavior and regain control of your life.

Additionally, "The Wizard of Oz and Other Narcissists" by Eleanor Payson explores the impact of narcissism on relationships and provides valuable insights into healing.

To further support your healing journey, consider reading "Complex PTSD: From Surviving to Thriving" by Pete Walker.

This book offers valuable insights into complex trauma and provides strategies for healing and recovering from the effects of abuse. "The Body Keeps the Score" by Bessel van der Kolk is another recommended resource that explores the impact of trauma on the body and provides a holistic approach to healing.

In addition to books specifically focused on narcissism and abuse recovery, it's important to expand your knowledge of personal growth and empowerment.

"The Power of Now" by Eckhart Tolle guides readers towards living in the present moment and finding inner peace, while "Rising Strong" by Brené Brown explores the transformative power of vulnerability and resilience.

Beyond books, there are other valuable resources and support systems available to assist you on your healing journey.

Online communities and support groups provide a safe space to connect with others who have experienced similar challenges and gain valuable insights and support.

Therapeutic modalities such as cognitive-behavioral therapy (CBT), dialectical behavior therapy (DBT), and eye movement desensitization and reprocessing (EMDR) can be beneficial in addressing trauma and supporting your healing process.

Remember, everyone's healing journey is unique, and it's important to find the resources and support systems that resonate with you personally.

Celebrate the moments when you actively seek out these resources and engage in self-care practices that nourish your mind, body, and soul.

In conclusion, Chapter 15 offers you a wealth of resources and support to enhance your knowledge and aid you on your path to healing and personal growth.

The recommended books provide valuable insights into narcissism, abuse recovery, and personal empowerment.

Additionally, online communities, therapy modalities, and self-care practices are essential components of your healing journey.

Embrace the moments when you explore these resources and utilize the support systems available to you, as they will empower you to navigate the challenges of narcissistic abuse and achieve true healing and transformation.

Online Resources and Support Groups: Introducing online platforms, forums, and support groups where survivors can connect with others who have experienced narcissistic abuse, share their stories, and receive support and validation.

Welcome to Chapter 15, where we explore the invaluable world of online resources and support groups for survivors of narcissistic abuse.

In this digital age, online platforms, forums, and support groups have become powerful tools for connecting with others who have experienced similar challenges, sharing stories, and finding support and validation.

Here, we highlight some of the prominent online resources that can offer solace and guidance on your healing journey.

One popular online platform is the "Narcissistic Abuse Recovery Forum," where survivors can find a community of individuals who understand their experiences.

This forum provides a safe space to share personal stories, seek advice, and receive emotional support from those who have walked a similar path.

The opportunity to connect with others who have firsthand knowledge of narcissistic abuse can be incredibly validating and empowering.

Another noteworthy online resource is the "Psych Central Narcissistic Abuse Support Group."

This group offers a supportive environment for survivors to discuss their experiences, ask questions, and receive guidance from mental health professionals and fellow survivors.

The combination of professional expertise and lived experiences creates a well-rounded and informative space for healing.

In addition to these platforms, social media communities have emerged as powerful avenues for support and connection.

Facebook groups such as "Narcissistic Abuse Recovery" and "Healing from Narcissistic Abuse" bring together individuals who have undergone narcissistic abuse and are seeking understanding, validation, and healing.

These groups foster a sense of community and offer a platform to share resources, personal stories, and coping strategies.

It's important to approach online resources and support groups with caution and discernment.

While these platforms can be immensely beneficial, it's crucial to prioritize your safety and well-being.

Remember to engage with reputable and moderated groups, where administrators take measures to ensure a supportive and respectful environment.

Alongside online resources, seeking professional support from therapists, counselors, or coaches who specialize in narcissistic abuse can be instrumental in your healing journey.

These professionals possess the knowledge and expertise to guide you through the process of navigating the complexities of narcissistic abuse and rebuilding your life.

In conclusion, Chapter 15 emphasizes the power of online resources and support groups in providing a sense of community, validation, and guidance for survivors of narcissistic abuse.

Platforms such as forums and social media groups offer a safe space to connect with others, share experiences, and seek support.

However, it's essential to exercise caution and choose reputable platforms that prioritize safety and well-being.

Remember, the online realm is just one aspect of your support network, and seeking professional guidance is equally important.

By combining online resources with professional support, you can embark on a healing journey that empowers you to navigate the aftermath of narcissistic abuse and reclaim your life.

Professional Organizations and Therapists: Listing reputable organizations and therapists specializing in narcissistic abuse recovery, providing readers with access to professional help and guidance.

Welcome to Chapter 15, where we explore the valuable resources and support available through professional organizations and therapists specializing in narcissistic abuse recovery.

When navigating the challenging aftermath of narcissistic abuse, seeking professional help and guidance can be a crucial step towards healing and reclaiming your life.

In this section, we will highlight reputable organizations and therapists that specialize in supporting survivors of narcissistic abuse.

One esteemed organization dedicated to this cause is the International Society for Narcissistic Abuse Recovery (ISNAR). ISNAR provides a wealth of information, resources, and support for individuals who have experienced narcissistic abuse.

Their website offers articles, educational materials, and access to trained professionals who can offer specialized guidance on healing from narcissistic abuse.

ISNAR's commitment to raising awareness and providing comprehensive support makes them a valuable resource for survivors.

In addition to organizations, seeking therapy or counseling from professionals with expertise in narcissistic abuse recovery can significantly aid in your healing journey.

A renowned therapist in this field is Dr. Linda Martinez-Lewi, a licensed clinical professional counselor and author specializing in narcissistic abuse recovery.

Her extensive knowledge and experience in working with survivors of narcissistic abuse make her a trusted guide in navigating the complexities of healing and moving forward.

Another reputable therapist is Shahida Arabi, a licensed counselor and bestselling author specializing in narcissistic abuse recovery.

Shahida's compassionate approach and wealth of knowledge have earned her recognition as an expert in the field.

Through her counseling services and writings, she offers survivors practical strategies and empowerment tools to rebuild their lives after narcissistic abuse.

When selecting a therapist, it's essential to find someone who resonates with you and whose approach aligns with your needs.

The Psychology Today website is a valuable resource to search for therapists specializing in narcissistic abuse recovery in your area.

Their directory provides detailed profiles of therapists, including their areas of expertise, treatment approaches, and contact information, making it easier to find a professional who suits your specific requirements.

It's crucial to remember that healing from narcissistic abuse is a deeply personal journey, and there is no one-size-fits-all approach.

Finding the right therapist or counselor who understands narcissistic abuse dynamics and has experience in this field can provide invaluable guidance and support.

In conclusion, Chapter 15 highlights the significance of professional organizations and therapists in the recovery process from narcissistic abuse.

Reputable organizations like ISNAR offer comprehensive resources and support, while therapists such as Dr. Linda Martinez-Lewi and Shahida Arabi specialize in helping survivors navigate the complexities of narcissistic abuse.

Remember to take the time to find a therapist who resonates with you and whose expertise aligns with your needs.

With the help of these professional resources, you can embark on a healing journey that empowers you to navigate and overcome the effects of narcissistic abuse, leading to a brighter and more fulfilling future.

Self-Help Tools and Apps: Recommending helpful tools, apps, and digital resources that can aid in the healing process, including meditation apps, self-care planners, and mental health resources.

In Chapter 15 of "Unmasking Narcissism: Empowering Strategies to Navigate and Heal from Narcissistic Abuse," we delve into the wealth of self-help tools and apps that can complement your healing journey.

These digital resources can provide valuable support, guidance, and empowerment as you navigate the recovery process from narcissistic abuse.

From meditation apps to self-care planners and mental health resources, incorporating these tools into your daily routine can contribute to your overall well-being and assist you in reclaiming your life.

When it comes to meditation apps, one highly recommended option is Calm.

Calm offers a variety of guided meditations, sleep stories, and breathing exercises specifically designed to reduce anxiety, promote relaxation, and cultivate mindfulness.

Its user-friendly interface and extensive library of content make it an excellent choice for individuals seeking a moment of peace and serenity amidst the challenges of healing from narcissistic abuse.

For those looking to prioritize self-care and maintain a structured routine, self-care planners can be incredibly helpful.

The Self-Care Planner is a popular digital tool that allows you to track and plan your self-care activities, set goals, and monitor your progress.

It provides a comprehensive framework to ensure that you are prioritizing your well-being and engaging in activities that nourish your mind, body, and soul.

Additionally, there are various mental health resources available online that can further support your healing journey.

The National Domestic Violence Hotline provides confidential support and resources for individuals experiencing domestic abuse, including narcissistic abuse.

Their website offers valuable information, safety planning guides, and access to trained advocates who can offer support and guidance.

Another noteworthy resource is the Narcissistic Abuse Recovery YouTube channel.

This channel features videos by survivors and experts sharing their experiences, insights, and strategies for healing from narcissistic abuse.

It serves as a virtual community where individuals can find validation, support, and practical advice from those who have walked a similar path.

When exploring self-help tools and apps, it's important to find what resonates with you personally.

Experiment with different resources and see which ones align with your needs and preferences.

Remember, everyone's healing journey is unique, so it's essential to find the tools that empower and resonate with you.

In conclusion, Chapter 15 of "Unmasking Narcissism: Empowering Strategies to Navigate and Heal from Narcissistic Abuse" introduces a range of self-help tools and apps to complement your healing journey.

Meditation apps like Calm, self-care planners, and mental health resources such as the National Domestic Violence Hotline and the Narcissistic Abuse Recovery YouTube channel offer valuable support and guidance. Incorporating these digital resources into your daily routine can contribute to your overall well-being and assist you in navigating and overcoming the effects of narcissistic abuse.

Remember to explore and find the tools that work best for you, empowering you to heal and thrive on your path to recovery.

Conclusion

Recap of Key Points and Steps for Handling a Narcissist and Healing from Narcissistic Abuse: Summarizing the essential steps and strategies discussed throughout the book.

In conclusion, "Unmasking Narcissism: Empowering Strategies to Navigate and Heal from Narcissistic Abuse" offers a comprehensive guide to understanding and addressing narcissistic abuse.

Throughout the book, we have explored various topics and strategies aimed at helping individuals regain their power, rebuild their lives, and heal from the detrimental effects of narcissistic relationships.

Let's recap the key points and steps for handling a narcissist and navigating the journey of healing from narcissistic abuse.

- Recognizing the Signs: The first step in addressing narcissistic abuse is to understand the signs and dynamics of narcissistic behavior.
- By familiarizing yourself with the characteristics and manipulation tactics employed by narcissists, you can gain clarity and validation for your experiences.
- Setting Boundaries: Establishing and enforcing healthy boundaries is crucial when dealing with a narcissist.
- Learning to say "no" and assert your needs helps protect your well-being and prevent further abuse.
- Seeking Support: Connecting with others who have

experienced narcissistic abuse can provide a valuable support network.

- Support groups, therapy, and online communities can offer empathy, validation, and guidance as you navigate the healing process.
- Practicing Self-Care: Prioritizing self-care is essential for your emotional, mental, and physical well-being.
- Engaging in activities that promote self-nurturing, self-reflection, and self-compassion can aid in your recovery journey.
- Healing Trauma: Addressing the trauma caused by narcissistic abuse requires professional help.
- Trauma-focused therapy, such as cognitive-behavioral therapy (CBT) or EMDR, can assist in processing and resolving the emotional wounds inflicted by the narcissistic relationship.
- Building Resilience: Cultivating resilience is key to thriving after narcissistic abuse.
- Engaging in practices such as mindfulness, positive affirmations, and gratitude can help you develop inner strength and navigate future challenges with resilience and grace.
- Embracing Personal Growth: Shift your focus from the past to the present and future.
- Embrace opportunities for personal growth, explore your passions, and create a fulfilling life beyond the abuse.
- Protecting Children: If you have children, it is crucial to shield them from the negative influence of a narcissistic parent.
- Co-parenting strategies, clear communication, and providing age-appropriate support can help your children heal and develop healthy relationships.
- Throughout this journey, it is essential to remember that

healing takes time.

- Each individual's healing process is unique, and it's important to be patient and kind to yourself as you navigate the ups and downs of recovery.

The resources, strategies, and support mentioned in this book are tools to empower you on your healing path, but it is recommended to seek professional help and tailor your approach to your specific circumstances.

By incorporating these strategies and taking the necessary steps to address narcissistic abuse, you are reclaiming your power, finding your voice, and creating a life of authenticity and fulfillment.

Remember, you are not alone, and there is hope for a brighter future beyond the shadows of narcissistic abuse.

Stay committed to your healing journey, surround yourself with a supportive community, and embrace the resilience within you.

In conclusion, "Unmasking Narcissism: Empowering Strategies to Navigate and Heal from Narcissistic Abuse" serves as a valuable resource and guide for those seeking to break free from the grips of narcissistic abuse and embark on a journey of healing and self-discovery.

By recapitulating the key points and steps discussed throughout the book, individuals are equipped with the knowledge and tools necessary to navigate the complexities of narcissistic relationships and reclaim their lives.

Remember, healing is a gradual process, and each step taken brings you closer to a life of empowerment, authenticity, and resilience.

Seek support, practice self-care,

Encouragement for Readers on Their Journey to Recovery and Empowerment: Offering words of encouragement, resilience, and hope to readers as they embark on their healing journey.

In conclusion, "Unmasking Narcissism: Empowering Strategies to Navigate and Heal from Narcissistic Abuse" serves as a guiding light for individuals on their journey to recovery and empowerment.

Throughout this book, we have delved into the intricate dynamics of narcissistic abuse, provided strategies to navigate the challenges, and empowered readers to reclaim their lives.

As we wrap up this empowering journey, it is important to offer words of encouragement, resilience, and hope to readers as they embark on their healing path.

Recovering from narcissistic abuse is a courageous and transformative process.

It requires strength, self-compassion, and a commitment to self-care.

Remember that healing is not linear, and it's okay to have ups and downs along the way.

Embrace the progress you've made, no matter how small, and celebrate your resilience.

You are not alone on this journey.

Reach out to trusted friends, family members, or support groups who can offer a listening ear and understanding.

Sharing your experiences and emotions with others who have walked a similar path can provide a sense of validation and support.

As you move forward, focus on nurturing yourself and rebuilding your life on a foundation of authenticity and self-love.

Take time to explore your passions, interests, and goals.

Engage in activities that bring you joy and provide a sense of fulfillment.

Remember that healing is not just about moving on from the past; it's about embracing the present and creating a brighter future.

Embrace the lessons learned from your experiences and use them as stepping stones toward personal growth and empowerment.

While this book provides a wealth of information and strategies, it is essential to recognize that every healing journey is unique.

What works for one person may not work for another.

It's important to find the approaches and resources that resonate with you and adapt them to your specific circumstances.

Lastly, always prioritize your well-being.

Seek professional help if needed, such as therapy or counseling, to address any lingering emotional wounds.

Take advantage of the resources and support networks available to you, both online and offline.

"Unmasking Narcissism: Empowering Strategies to Navigate and Heal from Narcissistic Abuse" encourages you to embrace your inner strength, trust in your resilience, and believe in the possibility of a brighter future.

Your healing journey is an opportunity for growth, self-discovery, and empowerment.

May you find solace, validation, and the courage to forge ahead on your path to recovery. Remember, you have the power to overcome, thrive, and create a life filled with joy, authenticity, and inner peace.

Final Thoughts: Emphasizing the importance of self-compassion, self-care, and ongoing growth in maintaining healthy relationships and thriving after narcissistic abuse.

In the final chapters of "Unmasking Narcissism: Empowering Strategies to Navigate and Heal from Narcissistic Abuse," we have explored the intricate dynamics of narcissistic abuse and provided valuable strategies to navigate the challenges and reclaim one's life.

As we conclude this empowering journey, it is crucial to emphasize the importance of self-compassion, self-care, and ongoing growth in maintaining healthy relationships and thriving after narcissistic abuse.

One of the key takeaways from this book is the significance of self-compassion.

It is natural to blame oneself or carry feelings of shame and guilt after enduring narcissistic abuse.

However, it is essential to remember that the responsibility lies with the abuser, not the survivor.

Practicing self-compassion involves treating oneself with kindness, understanding, and forgiveness.

It means acknowledging the pain and trauma experienced and providing oneself with the love and care needed for healing.

Alongside self-compassion, prioritizing self-care is vital in the healing process.

Narcissistic abuse can leave deep emotional scars, and engaging in regular self-care activities can help restore balance and promote overall well-being.

This may involve setting boundaries, practicing mindfulness and relaxation techniques, engaging in hobbies and activities that bring joy, and seeking professional support when needed.

Self-care is not selfish; it is a necessary component of healing and maintaining healthy relationships.

Furthermore, ongoing personal growth is an integral part of thriving after narcissistic abuse.

Recognizing and challenging any residual negative patterns or beliefs that may have developed as a result of the abuse is essential.

This may involve seeking therapy or counseling to address trauma, learning effective communication skills, and setting healthy boundaries.

It is an opportunity to redefine oneself, strengthen resilience, and cultivate a greater sense of self-worth.

As we conclude this journey, it is important to acknowledge that healing is a unique and individual process.

What works for one person may not work for another.

It requires patience, self-reflection, and a commitment to personal growth.

Surrounding oneself with a supportive network of friends, family, or support groups can provide encouragement, validation, and guidance along the way.

In summary, "Unmasking Narcissism: Empowering Strategies to Navigate and Heal from Narcissistic Abuse" emphasizes the significance of self-compassion, self-care, and ongoing growth in maintaining healthy relationships and thriving after narcissistic abuse.

By practicing self-compassion, prioritizing self-care, and embracing personal growth, survivors can reclaim their lives, break free from the cycle of abuse, and create fulfilling and healthy relationships.

*Remember,
your journey to
healing is unique,
and it is never too
late to embark
on the path of
empowerment,
resilience,
and personal transformation.*

Ingram Content Group UK Ltd.
Milton Keynes UK
UKHW020739070623
423023UK00014B/631